The Gnomean Book of Proverbs

Teachings and Reflections of the Church of Gnome

Written by:
Brett Larsen

Gnomean Elder of the Church of Gnome

2025

Introduction

This book is not a manual of rules, nor a tidy collection of solutions. It is a field of lanterns. Each proverb is one flame. Each reflection is another flame lit from it. Together they cast a glow, sometimes steady, sometimes flickering, on the winding path of human life.

The Church of Gnome was founded on the belief that wisdom does not belong to any one people, tradition, or doctrine. Wisdom is scattered like seeds across the earth. Some fall in scripture, some in science, some in laughter, some in grief. Some sprout in gardens. Some hide in the absurd. Our task is not to own it, but to notice it, tend to it, and share it when it grows. This book is one such harvest.

Proverbs within Proverbs

You will notice that each proverb is followed by a reflection. I wrote them as expansions, as deeper echoes. They are proverbs within the proverb; not explanations so much as invitations to linger, to let the initial spark burn a little longer. Sometimes they clarify; sometimes they complicate. They are not there to box in meaning, but to remind us that wisdom unfolds in layers, like a seed opening into root and stem, like a song returning to its chorus with new depth each time.

Poetry, Song, and the Creative Path

My own life has been shaped by poetry and song. Long before I became the Gnomean Elder, I was scribbling verses in notebooks, crafting lyrics late into the night, listening for rhythms that carried more truth than plain speech could. Songwriting taught me the value of repetition, the power of metaphor, the way a single image can hold an entire world. Many of the exercises that produced these proverbs began as poetic practices; free-writing until something broke open, turning overheard phrases into wisdom, or following a melody until it revealed a line I had not known I was carrying.

Poetry allowed me to hold contradictions without fear. Song taught me to honor cadence as much as content. Both became the soil where these proverbs grew.

The Two-Year Journey

This book took shape over the course of nearly two years. Some lines came to me in the whispers of the forest, while others arrived in the middle of the night when stillness opened the way for reflection. Inspiration arrived from many places; the quiet wonders of everyday life, the laughter shared with loved ones, the turning of the seasons, and, at times, the weight of sorrow or struggle. I began to see wisdom in the fragile power of an apology, in the double edge of silence that can hold us close or keep us apart. Some proverbs were born from witnessing the pain of the world in the news, yet just as many came from witnessing compassion, resilience, and joy shared among people.

In all of these experiences, I tried to listen. Not to force wisdom into words, but to receive it when it appeared. The proverbs are not inventions so much as recognitions. They surfaced when I paid attention; to pain and beauty, to shadow and light, to the full and ordinary miracle of being alive.

Repetition with Intention

You will notice that some themes return again and again. A single year cannot pass without us being asked to forgive more than once, to grieve more than once, to rest more than once, to remember our unity more than once. These proverbs mirror that truth. Some return gently, spread across months. Others come back-to-back, drilling a lesson into our hearts the way life itself sometimes does when we refuse to learn the first time. Repetition is not redundancy; it is rhythm. It is the pulse of wisdom, steady and insistent.

Metaphor, Mystery, and Freedom

Throughout these pages you will find metaphor interwoven with fact. A river may speak of grief. A lantern may speak of community. A squirrel may speak nonsense that, in its absurdity, reveals truth. This is not a flaw but a feature of wisdom. For metaphor often carries what direct speech cannot.

Here you are not asked to believe any one thing. The Church of Gnome does not force dogma upon you. We say instead: take what resonates, leave what does not. Let the words that meet you become companions. Let the ones that do not pass by like strangers. Spiritual freedom is as sacred to us as spiritual curiosity.

The Role of the Church of Gnome

The Church of Gnome was born from a conviction that the sacred is both profound and absurd, that mystery is not diminished by humor, and that the smallest symbols; a gnome in a garden, a strange hat upon a head; can open the largest questions.

Our mission is to nurture inner peace, to cultivate gratitude, to honor nature, to protect the sovereignty of body and mind, and to celebrate the bonds of community and companionship. This book of proverbs is not separate from that mission. It is one of its foundations.

In the same way that sacred texts across history have offered daily words of guidance, this book is offered as a companion for the Gnomean path. It does not stand alone, but alongside our principles, doctrine, rituals, and practices. Together they form a web of meaning that supports our lives, not by dictating how we must live, but by reminding us to live attentively, humbly, and with joy.

About the Author

I write this not only as the founder of the Church but as a human being who has known loss, love, doubt, and wonder. I have buried loved ones, wrestled with questions that have no answers, laughed until tears fell, and stood in silence before mysteries too large to name. Out of these experiences, the proverbs arose.

I am a father. A husband. A seeker. A friend. The Gnomean Elder. None of these titles capture the whole of me, but all of them flow into these pages.

The Purpose of this Book

The purpose of this book is simple but not small: to walk with you through the year. To be a lantern you can return to daily, or a field you can wander when you need guidance, comfort, or perspective. To offer you both the profound and the absurd, because both are sacred.

This book is not an endpoint. It is a companion. A mirror. A reminder. A seedbed.

A Blessing for the Reader

As you open these pages, may you treat them as a garden. Some paths will feel familiar. Others may seem strange. Some will confuse you at first, only to bloom later in memory. That is the way of proverbs. That is the way of life.

May these lanterns guide you not toward conformity but toward deeper presence.
May they remind you that wisdom is everywhere, if we learn to notice it.
And may they teach you that the light of one lantern does not diminish another; it only makes the path brighter.

Welcome. The lanterns are lit. The path is before you.

The light of one lantern does not diminish another; it only makes the path brighter.

When one flame joins another, the darkness loses its grip.
Shadows shrink, and the road ahead becomes clear.
The glow does not compete. It multiplies.

This Gnomean Proverb reminds us that what we give away is not lost.
Wisdom, compassion, love; these are not depleted by sharing.
They are magnified, made stronger by their passage from one soul to another.

At the Church of Gnome, we believe that every lantern is needed.
No single flame can carry the whole journey.
But together, the path becomes safe for all.
Light is meant to travel hand to hand, heart to heart.

Your lantern shines, and another joins it.
Neither is diminished.
Both are made brighter.
And the way forward is revealed.

Gnome Blessings.

Beneath every hat, gnome or not, is just a person doing their best.

The surface may carry colors, shapes, or symbols.
The face may wear pride or wear struggle.
But under it all is the same quiet truth: a being trying to find their way.

This Gnomean Proverb reminds us that judgment is easy when we stop at appearances.
Compassion is harder, and holier, because it looks deeper.
The hat is real, but it is not the whole story.

At the Church of Gnome, we believe every life is a mixture of strength and frailty.
No one walks without weight.
No one moves without mistakes.
Yet every person is still reaching for light, still seeking to belong, still doing what they can.

Look past the hat.
See the soul.
Recognize yourself in the one you would dismiss.

We are all just people, doing our best.

Gnome Blessings.

A gnome lives not for the moment, but for the soil it becomes.

Every choice is a planting.
Every act is a seed laid into the earth of tomorrow.
The moment matters, but the ground it leaves behind matters more.

This Gnomean Proverb reminds us that legacy is not carved in stone, but cultivated in soil.
The garden remembers long after the gardener has gone.
The roots hold the story of how the earth was tended.

At the Church of Gnome, we believe true life is measured not in fleeting pleasures, but in what endures.
Joy is not abandoned, but it is joined with responsibility.
Presence is not diminished, but it is expanded to care for what comes after.

To live for the soil is to live with reverence.
To live for the soil is to understand that the moment is a gift, but tomorrow is a trust.

Let your life become good earth.
Let your days enrich what others will stand upon.

Gnome Blessings.

A gnome watches the sky not to escape the earth, but to remember why it matters.

The heavens call the gaze upward, but the pull is not to
abandon.
It is to return with deeper love for what lies beneath the feet.

This Gnomean Proverb reminds us that wonder does not steal
us from the world.
It roots us more firmly in it.
The stars inspire, but they also remind us of our place within
the whole.

At the Church of Gnome, we believe the sacred is not divided
between above and below.
The sky and the soil are partners.
To look upward is to renew devotion to what grows downward.
To dream is not to flee, but to bring beauty back into the ground
we tend.

Lift your eyes without leaving your place.
Let the sky remind you of the worth of the earth.
Let the vastness above teach you reverence for the life around
you.

The heavens do not diminish the soil.
They hallow it.

Gnome Blessings.

The brush heals where language cannot reach.

Some wounds are too deep for words, too tangled for reason.
Paint, color, and shape step in where the tongue falters.
The canvas becomes a place where silence speaks and
brokenness is held.

This Gnomean Proverb reminds us that healing often comes
through expression, not explanation.
Art carries the weight words cannot.
It translates ache into beauty, grief into motion, longing into
form.

At the Church of Gnome, we believe creativity is a spiritual act.
It is prayer without sound.
It is confession without judgment.
It is the soul's language, spoken directly to the world.

You do not need eloquence to be whole.
You only need courage to let your hands speak what your voice
cannot.
Let the brush remind you that healing is not always heard, but
it can always be made visible.

Gnome Blessings.

A gnome never argues with trolls, they live under bridges for a reason.

To meet them in their dwelling is to be pulled into darkness.
To wrestle in their mud is to lose sight of your own path.

This Gnomean Proverb reminds us that not every fight deserves
our presence.
Some words are designed to wound, not to understand.
Some voices echo only to feed their own noise.

At the Church of Gnome, we believe dignity is found not in
every reply, but in knowing when silence is the stronger truth.
You do not need to climb down into the shadows to prove your
light.
You do not need to argue with those who thrive on conflict to
affirm your peace.

The bridge is for crossing, not for dwelling.
Keep moving forward.
Let the trolls stay where they choose, and walk on in the clarity
they cannot touch.

Gnome Blessings.

Follow the pull, even when reason scoffs.

There are callings that cannot be explained by logic alone.
The heart knows what the mind resists.
The soul feels what the charts cannot map.

This Gnomean Proverb reminds us that intuition is not
foolishness.
It is wisdom that rises from deeper soil.
It is the whisper that guides when reason has grown blind.

At the Church of Gnome, we believe mystery has a rightful place
in our lives.
Not everything must be proven to be true.
Not everything must be understood to be trusted.
Sometimes the pull is the map, and courage is the only compass
required.

Do not fear what cannot be explained.
Do not dismiss what you feel simply because it is unseen.
The pull has led many before you, and it will not abandon you
now.

Follow it.
It knows the way.

Gnome Blessings.

Do not argue with a talking squirrel. You're already losing.

The moment you engage nonsense on its own terms, it has already won.
Absurdity does not need your logic; it only needs your attention.

This Gnomean Proverb reminds us that wisdom is not proven in every debate.
It is shown in discernment.
Not all things are worth your breath, your time, or your peace.

At the Church of Gnome, we believe the sacred often asks us to choose our battles carefully.
Energy is precious.
Not every distraction deserves to be fed.
Not every voice requires an answer.

The squirrel may chatter forever.
You are free to smile, to listen lightly, and then to walk away.
In refusing to fight where there is no victory, you have already won.

Gnome Blessings.

Gnomes know we are made of the same mud and mystery.

Clay shaped into form, spirit breathed into matter,
the ordinary and the infinite woven into one fragile body.

This Gnomean Proverb reminds us that we are not separate
from one another, nor from the earth that birthed us.
The mud is our common ground.
The mystery is our shared inheritance.

At the Church of Gnome, we believe unity is found in
remembering what lies beneath the surface.
Titles, appearances, possessions, these are passing.
But the mud binds us, and the mystery lifts us.
Together they remind us that every life is equally sacred.

To see another as lesser is to forget your own soil.
To treat another without reverence is to forget the mystery that
moves in you as well.

We are made of the same substance.
We are shaped by the same wonder.
And in that truth, there is no hierarchy, only kinship.

Gnome Blessings.

Gnomes bow to the strange before they bow to the known.

What is familiar comforts, but it rarely transforms.
It is the unfamiliar that unsettles, teaches, awakens.

This Gnomean Proverb reminds us that the sacred often wears
the cloak of strangeness.
Mystery does not fit neatly into what we already believe.
It stretches us, humbles us, and invites us into deeper sight.

At the Church of Gnome, we believe reverence is not limited to
what we understand.
The unknown is not an enemy.
The unusual is not a threat.
To bow before the strange is to honor the vastness beyond our
control.

The known may anchor you, but the strange will expand you.
The known may soothe you, but the strange will grow you.

Do not fear the unfamiliar.
Bow to it.
Let it show you the edges of your own horizon.

Gnome Blessings.

Even kindness that goes unnoticed leaves footprints.

A smile no one returns, a gesture no one names, a gift no one thanks.
Still the ground remembers.
Still the soul it touched carries the mark.

This Gnomean Proverb reminds us that kindness is never wasted.
It is not measured by recognition, but by presence.
The good you offer does not vanish into silence.
It imprints itself in ways you may never see.

At the Church of Gnome, we believe love is not an exchange.
It is a seed.
Some bloom where you can witness.
Others root themselves deep in hidden soil.
But all of them matter.

You may not be celebrated.
You may not be noticed.
But you are still shaping the world in ways the world cannot forget.

Give freely.
The footprints remain.

Gnome Blessings.

Judgment freezes people in stories they've outgrown.

It chains them to the moment of their worst mistake.
It binds them to the version they once were, refusing them the
dignity of change.

This Gnomean Proverb reminds us that to judge too harshly is
to deny the truth of becoming.
No one is a finished story.
Everyone is in motion.
To freeze them is to turn them into stone, when they are meant
to keep moving.

At the Church of Gnome, we believe forgiveness is not erasure
but release.
It loosens the grip of the past.
It makes room for the possibility of growth.
It honors the unfolding nature of every soul.

See the new story, not only the old.
Trust the river, not the stone.
And remember that you too are still becoming.

Gnome Blessings.

Facing your darkness teaches you how to hold another's.

What you name within yourself, you can embrace in others.
What you deny within yourself, you will reject in them.

This Gnomean Proverb reminds us that compassion begins in
self-honesty.
The shadows you face are not your enemies.
They are your teachers, showing you how to walk gently with
others who stumble too.

At the Church of Gnome, we believe that wholeness is not the
absence of darkness.
It is the courage to face it without fear.
To carry your own shadows with dignity is to create space
where others can bring theirs without shame.

When you tend your own hidden places, you are preparing your
hands to hold another's.
When you heal your own pain, you are softening your heart to
meet theirs.

Your darkness is not wasted.
It can become the ground of your greatest compassion.

Gnome Blessings.

Abandoning yourself politely is still abandonment.

It may look kind.
It may sound agreeable.
It may even be praised as selfless.
But it is still a betrayal.

This Gnomean Proverb reminds us that peace with others is
hollow if it costs you peace with yourself.
To silence your voice for harmony is not harmony.
To neglect your needs for approval is not virtue.

At the Church of Gnome, we believe true kindness never
demands self-erasure.
Love must include yourself to be love at all.
Respect must extend inward before it can flourish outward.

Do not confuse politeness with integrity.
Do not mistake self-denial for generosity.
To honor yourself is not selfish.
It is the root from which authentic love can grow.

Stand with yourself, even gently.
That too is sacred.

Gnome Blessings.

Belonging is not always found in people, sometimes it's in place.

A forest that feels like home.
A river that remembers your name.
A quiet room where your soul can finally rest.

This Gnomean Proverb reminds us that community is not the only sanctuary.
The earth itself holds spaces of welcome.
The wind, the stone, the soil, these too can carry you.

At the Church of Gnome, we believe that belonging is more than fitting in.
It is resonance, the deep sense that something recognizes you as its own.
Sometimes that recognition comes from a friend.
Sometimes it comes from the ground beneath your feet.

Do not despair if people do not always provide the home you long for.
The world is wide with places that can.
Belonging is not confined to human arms.

Sometimes the truest embrace is the land itself.

Gnome Blessings.

Be the soft earth where another may safely fall.

When someone stumbles, they do not need your judgment.
They need your gentleness.
They need to land in a place that will not break them further.

This Gnomean Proverb reminds us that compassion is not only
spoken, it is felt.
It is the kindness that catches another before despair hardens
into permanence.
It is the mercy that turns collapse into the beginning of
renewal.

At the Church of Gnome, we believe to be human is to fall often.
What matters is not how many times, but whether there is
ground soft enough to rise from again.
You can be that ground.
You can be the place where someone's shame loosens its grip
and courage takes root.

Be soil for another.
Be gentleness when the world has been unkind.
Be the reminder that falling does not end the story.

Gnome Blessings.

Not every seed is yours to harvest.

You may plant, water, nurture, and still never see the fruit.
Another hand may gather what you began.
Another season may hold what you once dreamed.

This Gnomean Proverb reminds us that effort is not wasted,
even when it is unseen.
The work you do ripples forward.
The seed does not forget your touch.

At the Church of Gnome, we believe meaning is found in
participation, not possession.
Life is too vast for one person to claim all the harvest.
Sometimes your role is to sow.
Sometimes it is to tend.
Sometimes it is simply to trust that growth happens beyond
your sight.

Release the need to own the outcome.
Trust the cycle of seasons.
Know that your labor still matters, even if the fruit belongs to
another.

Gnome Blessings.

Begin again, as many times as needed. That is the path.

Failure is not final.
Weariness is not the end.
Each sunrise carries the gift of renewal.

This Gnomean Proverb reminds us that starting over is not
weakness.
It is wisdom.
To rise again is to honor your persistence more than your
perfection.

At the Church of Gnome, we believe beginnings are sacred no
matter how many times they arrive.
Every attempt reshapes you.
Every return deepens your strength.
The path is not a single straight line, but a series of returns to
what matters.

Do not fear the reset.
Do not despise the second, the tenth, or the hundredth attempt.
Each time you begin again, you affirm that you are still alive,
still becoming.

That persistence is holiness.

Gnome Blessings.

Magic is not rare, it is rarely noticed.

It shimmers in the ordinary.
It hides in plain sight, waiting for eyes willing to see.
A bird's call.
A child's laughter.
The quiet breath that keeps you alive.

This Gnomean Proverb reminds us that the sacred is not elsewhere.
It is here.
It does not wait in distant stars, but pulses in every moment we overlook.

At the Church of Gnome, we believe reverence is an act of attention.
To notice is to awaken.
To awaken is to be transformed.
What once seemed common reveals itself as extraordinary.

Do not wait for miracles wrapped in thunder.
Look closer.
The magic has always been near.

Gnome Blessings.

A broken attempt teaches more than a perfect excuse.

To risk and fail is to be alive.
To avoid and justify is to wither quietly.

This Gnomean Proverb reminds us that courage is found in the trying, not the outcome.
Mistakes are teachers, not enemies.
Excuses are prisons, disguised as safety.

At the Church of Gnome, we believe stumbling forward is holier than standing still.
The world is shaped by those willing to act, not by those waiting until they are flawless.
Your imperfect effort carries more light than your perfect avoidance.

Do not be afraid of breaking.
Be afraid of never beginning.
Let your attempt be messy, fragile, even incomplete.
It will teach you more than silence ever could.

Gnome Blessings.

Create the quiet where your soul can speak again.

The world is loud, and its noise seeps into your bones.
It fills the spaces where stillness should live.
It drowns the voice you most need to hear.

This Gnomean Proverb reminds us that silence is not
emptiness.
It is sanctuary.
It is the place where the deeper self rises and is finally heard.

At the Church of Gnome, we believe the soul is not absent.
It is often only hidden beneath the weight of endless sound.
When you choose quiet, you uncover what has been waiting all
along.

Let stillness return to you.
Let the silence carry wisdom.
In the hush, your own truth becomes clear.

Gnome Blessings.

Benevolence with conditions is just control in a softer voice.

What looks like kindness can mask a hidden chain.
What sounds like generosity can still be a demand.

This Gnomean Proverb reminds us that true giving is free of hooks.
It does not bind the receiver.
It does not demand repayment.
It lets go without expectation.

At the Church of Gnome, we believe love cannot be traded like currency.
Compassion is not leverage.
Mercy is not a disguise for power.
To give and still hold control is not to give at all.

If your hand offers while your heart keeps score, the gift is already broken.
Release the conditions.
Let kindness be clean, untangled, and whole.

Gnome Blessings.

Intuition is not a guess, it is ancestral memory rising.

It is the echo of those who came before.
It is wisdom carried in the marrow, surfacing when reason falls short.

This Gnomean Proverb reminds us that knowing often precedes proof.
There is a current beneath thought that pulls toward truth.
It is older than words, older than logic, older than you.

At the Church of Gnome, we believe intuition is sacred inheritance.
The ancestors live on in the signals of your body, the tug in your spirit, the quiet certainty that defies explanation.
To dismiss it is to cut yourself off from your own roots.

Trust the rising.
Trust the whisper.
Trust that what feels ancient in you is not mistake, but memory.

Gnome Blessings.

Beware the soil that flatters your feet but hides its thorns.

Not every welcome is genuine.
Not every comfort is safe.
Some ground invites you in only to wound you when you settle.

This Gnomean Proverb reminds us that discernment is as holy
as trust.
You are not asked to harden your heart, but to keep your eyes
open.
You are not asked to walk in fear, but to recognize what
pretends to be shelter.

At the Church of Gnome, we believe wisdom is the balance of
openness and caution.
Love freely, but see clearly.
Step gently, but do not ignore the ground you walk upon.

If the soil wounds while it praises, do not linger.
Your roots deserve a safer place to grow.

Gnome Blessings.

Death is not the end. It is a rearranging.

The form changes, but the essence remains.
The body falls, but the energy continues, reshaped and rejoined to the whole.

This Gnomean Proverb reminds us that endings are not erasures.
They are transformations.
What once walked beside you may now walk within you, around you, through the unseen.

At the Church of Gnome, we believe grief is real, and so is continuity.
The soil receives, the air releases, the spirit reshapes itself into new forms of presence.
Love does not vanish at the grave.
It rearranges into memory, into guidance, into the invisible threads that still bind us.

Do not fear the rearranging.
It is not loss but movement.
Not silence but another kind of song.

Death is not an absence.
It is a reweaving.

Gnome Blessings.

Not every locked door is meant to open. Some are there to keep the wind out.

The barrier that frustrates you may also be the wall that protects you.
The unopened path may be the one that saves you from harm.

This Gnomean Proverb reminds us that not all obstacles are punishments.
Sometimes they are boundaries set in wisdom.
Sometimes they are mercies disguised as refusals.

At the Church of Gnome, we believe discernment is found in knowing when to push and when to turn away.
Not every closed door demands your effort.
Not every barrier asks to be broken.
Some are simply there to keep you warm, safe, and whole.

Do not waste your strength forcing what is not meant to open.
Trust that protection is sometimes hidden in disappointment.
The wind was never meant to own you.

Gnome Blessings.

A seed is a prayer written in dirt.

Small, silent, and unseen, yet carrying an entire future.
Buried in darkness, it waits for light, water, and time.

This Gnomean Proverb reminds us that hope often begins hidden.
It is not loud.
It is not immediate.
It is patient, trusting the soil to guard what it cannot yet reveal.

At the Church of Gnome, we believe prayer is not only spoken.
It is planted.
Every act of kindness.
Every risk of love.
Every dream surrendered to time is a seed entrusted to the earth.

Do not despise what seems small.
It may already contain what you most long for.
Wait, and let the soil do its work.

Gnome Blessings.

The garden needs every shape of root.

Some spread wide.
Some reach deep.
Some tangle together in ways that seem chaotic, yet all are
essential.

This Gnomean Proverb reminds us that diversity sustains life.
There is no single right way to belong.
There is no single root that carries all the weight.

At the Church of Gnome, we believe each life adds something
the whole would lack without it.
Strength is not found in uniformity, but in the weaving
together of differences.
Every root contributes to the nourishment of the garden.

Do not compare your growth to another.
Do not shrink because your roots look different.
The garden is wide enough for them all.

Gnome Blessings.

The moon does not speak, yet every gnome knows its language.

It shines without words.
It guides without noise.
Its silence is full of meaning.

This Gnomean Proverb reminds us that not all truth is carried in speech.
Some truths are felt, not spoken.
Some languages are older than words.

At the Church of Gnome, we believe listening goes beyond the ear.
It is the openness of the heart.
It is the willingness to receive what cannot be explained, yet cannot be denied.

The moon teaches that silence can be eloquent.
That stillness can be guiding.
That light, even without sound, can tell the deepest stories.

Learn to listen beyond language.
The world has more to say than words can hold.

Gnome Blessings.

Closure doesn't require their voice, only your truth.

You may wait forever for the apology that never comes.
You may long for words that will not arrive.
But your healing does not depend on their permission.

This Gnomean Proverb reminds us that freedom begins within.
You are not bound to someone else's silence.
You are not imprisoned by what they refuse to give.

At the Church of Gnome, we believe your truth is enough to set you free.
You can name what happened.
You can honor the wound.
And you can choose to step forward without waiting for their blessing.

Closure is not a gift they can give.
It is a decision you make.
It is the courage to carry your own voice when theirs has failed.

Your truth is sufficient.
Your healing is already in motion.

Gnome Blessings.

You are not a character, you are the narrator.

The role others place you in is not your prison.
The script they hand you is not your destiny.
The voice that tells the story belongs to you.

This Gnomean Proverb reminds us that life is not a stage to be
endured, it is a story to be authored.
You are not confined to someone else's version of who you are.
You are free to tell the truth differently, to name yourself in
your own words.

At the Church of Gnome, we believe sovereignty begins with
story.
The past may shape the chapters, but you decide the meaning.
The future may carry unknown pages, but you choose how the
tale unfolds.

Do not confuse yourself with a part you were cast to play.
You are the voice that shapes it all.
Speak with courage, and watch the story change.

Gnome Blessings.

To create is to speak the sacred in a tongue older than words.

Every line of paint, every carved form, every melody rising from silence is a translation of mystery.
The sacred does not wait only in temples; it moves through hands, breath, and imagination.

This Gnomean Proverb reminds us that creativity is not luxury, but prayer.
It is communion with something vast.
It is humanity joining its voice to the chorus that has always been.

At the Church of Gnome, we believe creation is revelation.
When you make, you echo the original Maker.
When you give form to beauty, you remind the world of its own divine roots.

Do not underestimate your craft.
Every act of creation is a holy conversation.
Every stroke of the hand is a sentence in the language of eternity.

Gnome Blessings.

A true apology is an offering, not a transaction.

It is not a bargaining chip.
It is not a tool to restore your image.
It is the laying down of pride so that trust can begin to grow again.

This Gnomean Proverb reminds us that apology is not owed, it is given.
It does not demand forgiveness.
It does not insist on reconciliation.
It simply honors the truth of harm and the hope of repair.

At the Church of Gnome, we believe apology is sacred.
It is a form of humility that restores dignity where it was taken.
It is the soft soil where healing can take root.

Apologize not to clear your conscience, but to honor the one who was hurt.
Offer your words as gift, not currency.
That is where restoration begins.

Gnome Blessings.

Heal now so the future doesn't have to bleed for it.

The wound you ignore does not disappear.
It waits, growing sharper, pressing itself into tomorrow's
veins.

This Gnomean Proverb reminds us that healing deferred is
suffering multiplied.
What you do not face, the future must carry.
What you refuse to mend, your children, your friends, your own
older self may inherit.

At the Church of Gnome, we believe healing is not selfish work,
it is generational mercy.
When you tend your pain, you are tending the soil others will
walk upon.
When you stitch your wounds, you prevent them from tearing
new skin later.

Do not delay.
Do not bury what aches.
Heal now, so that what is to come is freed from carrying what
you left undone.

Gnome Blessings.

A gnome leaves berries for those who haven't arrived yet.

They think of the unseen traveler.
They prepare for the one they may never meet.
Their gift is for the future, not for applause.

This Gnomean Proverb reminds us that generosity is not always about what is returned.
It is about planting kindness where someone else may find it later.
It is about offering sustenance you may never witness being received.

At the Church of Gnome, we believe true giving is timeless.
It stretches beyond the moment, beyond the giver, beyond the need you can see.
It creates pathways of grace for those who will walk long after you are gone.

Leave something behind.
A kindness.
A gift.
A sign that someone once thought of them.

The berries you leave may become the hope that carries another forward.

Gnome Blessings.

In the hush of night, the veil lifts inwards.

Silence settles, distractions fade, and what has been waiting
beneath the noise rises to the surface.
The sacred does not always come with thunder.
Sometimes it comes with a whisper only stillness can hear.

This Gnomean Proverb reminds us that the deepest truths are
not found by straining outward.
They are found by softening inward.
The night invites reflection, drawing you closer to your own
center, where the veil is thinnest.

At the Church of Gnome, we believe the inward journey is as
holy as the outward search.
To turn within is not escape.
It is contact with the eternal dwelling inside you.

In the hush, listen.
In the hush, remember.
In the hush, find that the veil was never keeping you out, only
guiding you in.

Gnome Blessings.

Peace begins where control ends.

The more you grasp, the more it slips away.
The more you demand, the more restless your spirit becomes.

This Gnomean Proverb reminds us that peace is not earned
through domination.
It is received through release.
It grows in the soil of trust, not in the clenched fist of certainty.

At the Church of Gnome, we believe surrender is not defeat.
It is wisdom.
To stop forcing is to let harmony return.
To let go is to let life move in its natural rhythm.

When control ends, peace has room to breathe.
When striving ceases, the heart finally rests.
Let the grip loosen.
Peace is waiting.

Gnome Blessings.

Compassion doesn't mean staying. It means understanding while walking away.

Love can honor another without tethering yourself to harm.
Mercy can remain even when closeness cannot.

This Gnomean Proverb reminds us that compassion is not captivity.
It does not demand you endure what diminishes you.
It asks you to see clearly, to wish well, and still to step away when needed.

At the Church of Gnome, we believe boundaries are sacred.
They protect both the one who sets them and the one who inspired them.
They say: I honor your humanity, but I will not lose mine in the process.

Compassion is strongest when it is honest.
And sometimes honesty says goodbye.

Gnome Blessings.

A garden cannot bloom if the gardener never sits to smell the soil.

Endless labor without pause robs the joy from the harvest.
Growth becomes burden when beauty is never received.

This Gnomean Proverb reminds us that life is not only for tending.
It is also for savoring.
The work is sacred, but so is the rest that lets you notice what has been created.

At the Church of Gnome, we believe presence is as important as productivity.
To sit among your efforts is to honor them.
To breathe in their fragrance is to remember why you began in the first place.

Do not only plant.
Do not only toil.
Pause long enough to love what is already here.

Gnome Blessings.

Each recollection is a prayer to the version of you who survived.

Memory is not just remembering.
It is honoring.
It is gratitude whispered to the self that kept going when it
could have stopped.

This Gnomean Proverb reminds us that survival is sacred.
Looking back is not weakness.
It is recognition.
It is saying thank you to the one who endured enough to deliver
you here.

At the Church of Gnome, we believe resilience deserves
reverence.
Your past self deserves to be seen, not forgotten.
Every scar is proof of passage.
Every recollection is an altar built to endurance.

When you remember, bow gently to the one who carried you.
They were not perfect, but they were faithful.
You are here because of them.

Gnome Blessings.

Reacting defends. Reflecting transforms.

The quick response may shield you, but it rarely changes you.
It protects the surface while leaving the roots untouched.

This Gnomean Proverb reminds us that reflection takes courage.
It asks you to pause, to look inward, to meet yourself honestly.
In that pause, transformation begins.

At the Church of Gnome, we believe growth is found not in the speed of our reactions, but in the depth of our reflections.
The moment you reflect, you shift from survival to becoming.
You turn from the shield to the lantern.

Do not only defend yourself.
Learn from yourself.
Let reflection shape what reaction never could.

Gnome Blessings.

If you feel out of place, it means you were born to build a new one.

The discomfort is not proof of failure.
It is proof of calling.
It is the whisper that the world is not finished yet, and you are part of its making.

This Gnomean Proverb reminds us that belonging is not always found.
Sometimes it is created.
Sometimes the ache of not fitting is the very seed of a new home.

At the Church of Gnome, we believe misfits are often the builders of sanctuaries.
The world expands through those who refuse to accept that there is no room for them.
The ache of not belonging becomes the blueprint for a place where others will belong.

If you feel out of place, do not despair.
It means the world still needs the home only you can create.

Gnome Blessings.

The flame in you does not need permission to burn.

It does not wait for approval.
It does not require validation.
It exists because it is yours, because it was always meant to be.

This Gnomean Proverb reminds us that the inner fire is not
given by others, and therefore cannot be taken away by them.
The flame belongs to you.
Its worth is not determined by how it is received.

At the Church of Gnome, we believe each person carries a sacred
fire.
It is your passion, your truth, your essence.
It is your right to tend it, to let it shine, to let it warm the world
around you.

Do not smother it for fear of judgment.
Do not hide it for the sake of acceptance.
Your flame is already enough.
Let it burn.

Gnome Blessings.

A brownie blesses the corner where gratitude lingers.

Unseen, quiet, tucked in the hidden places of the home, the
brownie does not seek applause.
It responds instead to the atmosphere of thanks, to the warmth
of recognition given without demand.

This Gnomean Proverb reminds us that gratitude is what
sanctifies a space.
It invites blessing, whether through mythic hands or through
the subtle shift of the spirit.
Where complaint festers, blessing thins; where thanks abides,
blessing multiplies.

At the Church of Gnome, we believe unseen labor is as sacred as
the visible.
Every floor swept, every dish washed, every corner tended
becomes altar when done in gratitude.
The brownie's blessing is not fantasy; it is a truth disguised in
story, teaching us that gratitude draws goodness near.

Bless your corners.
Bless your tasks.
Bless your unseen helpers, within and without.

Gnome Blessings.

Sit with a stone long enough, and you'll hear its story.

At first there is silence.
Then patience reveals a rhythm.
The weight, the stillness, the memory it carries begin to speak.

This Gnomean Proverb reminds us that wisdom is not always immediate.
It unfolds slowly, through presence, through attention, through time.
The stone teaches what the hurried heart will always miss.

At the Church of Gnome, we believe listening is as holy as speaking.
The world is alive with voices that do not use words.
The earth carries stories older than any book.
To hear them, you must slow yourself to their pace.

When you sit long enough, silence becomes language.
And what seemed mute reveals it has always been speaking.

Gnome Blessings.

The sacred does not care if you believe in it. Only if you approach with wonder.

Mountains do not shrink because you doubt them.
The ocean does not lose depth because you question its
vastness.
Holiness remains, whether you name it or not.

This Gnomean Proverb reminds us that belief is not the
gatekeeper of mystery.
The sacred asks only that you notice, that you come close, that
you allow yourself to be moved.

At the Church of Gnome, we believe reverence belongs to all
people, regardless of creed.
The sacred does not demand allegiance.
It invites awe.
It waits in the soil, in the sky, in the pulse of your own being.

Do not worry about whether you believe enough.
Simply arrive with wonder.
That is all the sacred requires.

Gnome Blessings.

Inspiration visits, not to stay, but to move through you.

It is a guest, not a resident.
It comes quickly, unexpectedly, and it asks for your attention
before it fades.

This Gnomean Proverb reminds us that inspiration is not ours
to own.
It flows like water, passing from one to another.
It does not wait for convenience.
It asks to be welcomed, tended, and then released.

At the Church of Gnome, we believe inspiration is sacred
movement.
It is the breath of creation, stirring us into action.
To ignore it is to let the guest leave unwelcomed.
To honor it is to let beauty be born.

Do not cling to it.
Do not hoard it.
Let it pass through you, and you will know it was never yours
alone.

Gnome Blessings.

Name them. Bless them. Even if they never knew their gift.

Some people touch your life in ways they cannot see.
A word spoken in passing.
A kindness they forgot but you still remember.

This Gnomean Proverb reminds us that gratitude need not
always be received to be real.
You can honor someone in your heart, even if they never hear it.
You can bless their memory, even if they never knew the weight
of what they gave you.

At the Church of Gnome, we believe blessing ripples outward.
Every act of recognition strengthens the web of connection.
Every unspoken thank you carries power.
The world is quietly healed by these invisible offerings.

So name them.
Bless them.
Let your remembrance be prayer enough.

Gnome Blessings.

A single tear waters more than a thousand lectures.

What the mind resists, the heart receives.
Grief speaks a language stronger than arguments.
Compassion grows from what is felt, not only from what is taught.

This Gnomean Proverb reminds us that vulnerability is not weakness.
It is instruction in its purest form.
One honest emotion can soften what countless words could not.

At the Church of Gnome, we believe the soul learns best from authenticity.
Your tears teach courage.
Your tears teach empathy.
Your tears teach love in a way logic never could.

Do not hide them.
They are not failures.
They are lessons written in water.

Gnome Blessings.

Healing begins when you stop calling harm "just the way things are".

The wound cannot close if it is renamed as normal.
The cycle cannot end if it is excused as inevitable.

This Gnomean Proverb reminds us that change begins with honesty.
What is broken must be seen as broken.
What is unjust must be named as such.
Truth is the first medicine.

At the Church of Gnome, we believe resignation is not peace.
It is surrender to what harms.
Healing begins the moment you refuse to normalize pain.
It begins the moment you choose to tell the truth about what has been.

Do not call the wound natural.
Call it what it is, and let it mend.
The way things are does not need to be the way things remain.

Gnome Blessings.

A pet is not beneath you. They are beside you. Spirit wrapped in fur.

Their eyes carry memory older than words.
Their trust is not ownership, it is covenant.
Their presence is companionship in its purest form.

This Gnomean Proverb reminds us that sacredness is not
limited to humans.
The soul wears many forms.
Love speaks through paws, through feathers, through gentle
weight curled against you.

At the Church of Gnome, we believe pets are sacred companions
of spirit.
They teach loyalty without demand.
They offer comfort without judgment.
They remind us that life is best when shared across species, not
hoarded in one.

Do not think of them as lesser.
Think of them as fellow travelers.
Your paths are bound, and your spirits are kin.

Gnome Blessings.

Making peace means holding yourself with gentler hands.

The harshest wars are often fought within.
Criticism can become cruelty.
Perfection can become prison.

This Gnomean Proverb reminds us that peace is not only
something we extend outward.
It must begin inward.
The way you treat yourself shapes the way you move through
the world.

At the Church of Gnome, we believe self-compassion is the
foundation of all compassion.
To be gentle with yourself is to learn how to be gentle with
others.
To forgive your own wounds is to open space for forgiveness to
bloom everywhere.

Make peace with your own heart.
Hold yourself softly.
That gentleness is not indulgence.
It is survival.

Gnome Blessings.

The final breath carries all the unspoken thank yous.

Gratitude that never found its words still moves into the air.
Love withheld by fear or time still escapes in that release.

This Gnomean Proverb reminds us that nothing heartfelt is
ever fully lost.
Even the silences speak in the end.
The last breath carries them forward like prayer.

At the Church of Gnome, we believe death is not silence but
offering.
The final moment gathers all that could not be said and delivers
it into eternity.

Listen gently to the space after goodbye.
It is filled with thank yous too deep for words.

Gnome Blessings.

Even the dust between your fingers was once part of a star's prayer.

The smallest speck carries a story of fire, collapse, and rebirth.
What feels ordinary is born of the extraordinary.

This Gnomean Proverb reminds us that nothing is insignificant.
The cosmos lives within every grain of matter.
The divine breath lingers in the simplest particles.

At the Church of Gnome, we believe reverence is not only for
the vast.
It is for the tiny.
It is for the unnoticed.
It is for the dust that holds the memory of stars.

The universe is not elsewhere.
It is in your hands already.

Gnome Blessings.

The gnome tends the present with tomorrow in mind.

Every action is rooted in care for what comes next.
Every seed planted, every stone placed, every path cleared holds
a vision of the future.

This Gnomean Proverb reminds us that wisdom does not rush
past the moment, but neither does it forget what follows.
The present is precious, but it is also soil for tomorrow.
To tend it well is to honor both now and what is yet to be.

At the Church of Gnome, we believe stewardship is sacred.
We inherit the earth, but we also prepare it for those who will
come after us.
The present is not only ours to enjoy, it is ours to shape into a
gift.

Live now with joy.
Live now with care.
For tomorrow is already growing from today's hands.

Gnome Blessings.

To delight in another's fall is to loosen the ground beneath your own feet.

Cruelty may feel like triumph for a moment, but it corrodes the spirit that carries it.
Every laugh at another's misfortune cracks the foundation of compassion you yourself depend on.

This Gnomean Proverb reminds us that harm never remains contained.
It seeps into the one who celebrates it, dimming the lantern, souring the heart, and turning joy into poison.
What begins as mockery of another ends as instability within yourself.

At the Church of Gnome, we believe joy must never be built on another's pain.
True joy is expansive, multiplying without cost to anyone.
When we honor the dignity of others, even in their failings, we strengthen the dignity in ourselves.

Guard your ground.
Do not loosen it with cruel delight.
Keep your lantern bright with compassion.

Gnome Blessings.

Compassion does not require self-erasure.

Loving others should not mean abandoning yourself.
Mercy loses its holiness when it empties you beyond repair.

This Gnomean Proverb reminds us that kindness without balance becomes harm.
It is not compassion to destroy yourself for another's comfort.
It is not compassion to silence your truth for the sake of peace.

At the Church of Gnome, we believe real compassion includes both giver and receiver.
Your well-being matters as much as the one you love.
Your boundaries are not barriers; they are sacred lines that protect everyone involved.

Give, but not until you disappear.
Love, but not until you are lost.
True compassion holds both hearts at once.

Gnome Blessings.

Gnomes thrive in circles, not thrones.

They gather as equals, each voice valued, each hand
contributing.
The circle is where connection lives, where power is shared
instead of hoarded.

This Gnomean Proverb reminds us that community flourishes
through inclusion, not hierarchy.
The throne isolates.
The circle unites.

At the Church of Gnome, we believe belonging means standing
side by side, not above or below.
In the circle, no one is too small to matter.
No one is too mighty to listen.
The strength of the whole is found in its shared light.

Choose circles.
Choose gathering.
Choose the shape where love has no corners.

Gnome Blessings.

Every layer you peel back invites someone else to return to themselves.

Your honesty is a mirror.
Your vulnerability becomes permission.
Your courage to be real creates space for others to do the same.

This Gnomean Proverb reminds us that authenticity is contagious.
When one person sheds their mask, others remember they can too.
Your healing ripples outward, loosening chains you may never see.

At the Church of Gnome, we believe truth-telling is communal medicine.
The courage of one heart can restore many.
Every step toward your own wholeness clears a path for someone else.

Peel back what hides you.
Let your life become invitation.
Others are waiting for your example to guide them home.

Gnome Blessings.

Decay feeds roots you cannot see.

What looks like ending is often beginning.
What falls into the soil is not lost, but transformed.

This Gnomean Proverb reminds us that life is sustained by
cycles of loss.
The fallen leaf becomes food.
The broken branch becomes ground.
Death itself becomes the nourishment of future life.

At the Church of Gnome, we believe endings are not emptiness.
They are offerings.
They give rise to growth beyond what the eye can trace.

Do not fear the rot.
Do not despise the falling away.
The roots are being fed by what you cannot yet understand.

Trust the cycle.
Life is still unfolding beneath the surface.

Gnome Blessings.

Every soul is soil. Titles, robes and hats are just decoration.

The outer layers may mark status, but they do not make the
spirit.
What matters is the ground within, the fertile or barren places
of the heart.

This Gnomean Proverb reminds us that the sacred is not in
symbols alone.
They may point the way, but they are not the substance.
The soil of the soul is what gives life, what grows love, what
roots wisdom.

At the Church of Gnome, we believe reverence belongs to all,
not only to those who wear markers of honor.
Your worth is not stitched into garments.
It is alive in the soil of your being.

Tend the ground within you.
That is the true sanctuary.

Gnome Blessings.

You don't need permission to be what you already are.

The truth of your being is not granted by others.
It is not earned, not awarded, not approved.
It simply is.

This Gnomean Proverb reminds us that authenticity is not a negotiation.
It is birthright.
The soul does not wait for consent to exist.

At the Church of Gnome, we believe living honestly is sacred work.
The more you honor your essence, the more peace you carry.
The more you shrink for others, the more distance you create from yourself.

Stand in your being.
It was never theirs to permit.

Gnome Blessings.

Accept joy as the offering it is, not the debt it isn't.

Happiness is not repayment.
It is not proof that you have earned enough or suffered enough
to deserve it.
It is gift, freely given.

This Gnomean Proverb reminds us that joy does not require
justification.
To question it is to close your hands against what is already
yours.
To accept it is to honor the generosity of life.

At the Church of Gnome, we believe joy is holy.
It is meant to be received without suspicion.
It is sacred not because it balances suffering, but because it
exists at all.

Open your hands.
Let joy arrive without debt, without shame, without fear.

Gnome Blessings.

Ask before you judge, there's a story there.

Every face hides a journey.
Every action has a root.
What seems obvious from a distance often holds pain you
cannot see.

This Gnomean Proverb reminds us that judgment without
curiosity is blindness.
The story changes once you listen.
The truth expands once you ask.

At the Church of Gnome, we believe compassion is born from
questions, not conclusions.
To ask is to honor another's humanity.
To listen is to step into the mystery of who they are.

Do not settle for assumptions.
There is always more beneath the surface.
Ask, and let the story soften you.

Gnome Blessings.

A shaken belief can still stand if the roots are true.

Storms may bend it.
Questions may rattle it.
Doubt may shake it nearly to the ground.
Yet if the roots hold, it will endure.

This Gnomean Proverb reminds us that faith is not fragile.
Its strength is not in never being tested, but in surviving the test.
What is shallow will fall away, but what is rooted will remain.

At the Church of Gnome, we believe doubt is not the enemy of belief.
It is its companion.
It clears away the surface so that the roots can be seen.

Do not fear the shaking.
It proves what is real.
The roots are deeper than you think.

Gnome Blessings.

Not everyone deserves front row in your life.

Some are better loved from a distance.
Some are safest in the balcony, far from your vulnerable center.

This Gnomean Proverb reminds us that access is not
entitlement.
Your heart is not a public square.
It is a sacred space, and only some are meant to sit close.

At the Church of Gnome, we believe boundaries are holy.
They are not walls of bitterness, but gates of discernment.
To choose who sits near is not cruelty.
It is wisdom.

Offer kindness freely.
Offer access carefully.
Not all voices belong at the center of your stage.

Gnome Blessings.

Peace built on dishonesty cracks beneath your feet.

It may look solid for a time.
It may even carry weight briefly.
But eventually it splinters, leaving you unsteady.

This Gnomean Proverb reminds us that truth is the only ground
peace can grow upon.
Without it, harmony is a fragile illusion.
With it, peace becomes strong enough to endure storms.

At the Church of Gnome, we believe honesty is not the enemy of
peace, but its foundation.
The lie delays conflict, but it cannot prevent it.
The truth may be hard, but it creates space for peace that lasts.

Do not settle for fragile footing.
Choose truth, even when it trembles.
It is the only soil peace can grow in.

Gnome Blessings.

Their gaze reminds you that you were always enough.

Not because they complete you, but because they reveal what was already there.
Their love does not make you whole.
It simply uncovers your wholeness.

This Gnomean Proverb reminds us that the right presence does not fill your emptiness.
It reflects your fullness.
It does not give you worth.
It reminds you of the worth you carried all along.

At the Church of Gnome, we believe love's highest gift is not dependence, but recognition.
It turns the mirror toward you, showing what you had forgotten to see.

When someone's gaze restores you, it is not their magic you need to cling to.
It is your own truth, remembered in their eyes.

Gnome Blessings.

The more you laugh at your need to be important, the freer you become.

Ego loosens when met with humor.
Pride shrinks when you choose joy over performance.

This Gnomean Proverb reminds us that freedom is found in lightness.
The less you cling to being noticed, the more space you have to live fully.
Importance fades, but aliveness remains.

At the Church of Gnome, we believe humility is not humiliation.
It is liberation.
To laugh at yourself is to remind your soul that it was never chained to status.
It was always meant for play, for peace, for wonder.

Loosen the grip of needing to matter most.
In laughter, you will find you already matter enough.

Gnome Blessings.

To be different is to remind the world how wide the sacred really is.

Your uniqueness is not a mistake.
It is revelation.
It expands the vision of what holiness can look like.

This Gnomean Proverb reminds us that difference is not deficiency.
It is gift.
It stretches the world's understanding.
It widens the circle of belonging.

At the Church of Gnome, we believe the sacred is vast enough to hold every variation.
Every shade of being.
Every sound, shape, and way of living.
Each difference is another doorway into the holy.

Do not shrink to fit the narrow.
Stand as reminder.
You show the world how wide the sacred truly is.

Gnome Blessings.

Innovation without soul is just noise.

The new may dazzle for a moment, but without heart, it fades quickly.
Progress is not measured in speed, but in depth.

This Gnomean Proverb reminds us that creation without meaning cannot sustain.
What lacks spirit may entertain, but it will not endure.
What carries soul will echo far beyond its time.

At the Church of Gnome, we believe true innovation serves life.
It roots itself in compassion, in wisdom, in the sacred need to uplift.
Without soul, invention is clutter.
With soul, it becomes gift.

Do not chase novelty for its own sake.
Infuse your work with spirit, and it will last.

Gnome Blessings.

The past is not dead, it's whispering through you.

Its lessons move in your instincts.
Its wounds echo in your choices.
Its wisdom guides in ways you may not always see.

This Gnomean Proverb reminds us that the past is not gone; it is alive in memory and inheritance.
It breathes through your being.
It shapes you even as you shape the future.

At the Church of Gnome, we believe honoring the past does not mean being bound by it.
It means listening to its whispers without mistaking them for chains.
The past is teacher, not master.
It lives in you to guide, not to trap.

Hear its voice.
Learn its song.
Then walk forward carrying its wisdom lightly.

Gnome Blessings.

To commune with the cosmos, you need only stand still beneath it.

No temple required.
No words demanded.
Only your presence, your breath, your gaze lifted upward.

This Gnomean Proverb reminds us that the sacred is not distant.
It arches over you in every night sky.
It waits in the stars, patient for your attention.

At the Church of Gnome, we believe communion is not confined to ritual.
It can happen in a single moment of stillness.
It can happen in the vast silence between you and the infinite.

Stand still.
Look up.
The cosmos will meet you there.

Gnome Blessings.

If you cannot understand, be gentle.

Confusion is not an excuse for cruelty.
Ignorance is not license for harm.
The unknown calls for patience, not judgment.

This Gnomean Proverb reminds us that gentleness is the
answer when clarity is out of reach.
You may not grasp another's story, but you can still honor it.
You may not share another's pain, but you can still soften your
presence.

At the Church of Gnome, we believe gentleness is wisdom in
practice.
It fills the gaps where comprehension fails.
It bridges divides without needing full explanation.

When you cannot understand, choose kindness anyway.
That choice is its own form of knowing.

Gnome Blessings.

Don't plant onions and expect roses.

The harvest always matches the seed.
What you sow in bitterness will not blossom into sweetness.
What you plant in anger will not yield peace.

This Gnomean Proverb reminds us that cause and effect are
faithful companions.
The soil returns what is placed within it.
No one reaps joy from seeds of harm.

At the Church of Gnome, we believe accountability is woven
into creation itself.
To plant wisely is to live wisely.
To plant with care is to live with hope.

Examine your seeds.
Choose them with reverence.
For the garden always gives back what was sown.

Gnome Blessings.

The hidden self leaves breadcrumbs in every story you tell.

Even in laughter, the truth peeks through.
Even in silence, the longing speaks.
The self you try to conceal finds its way into your words.

This Gnomean Proverb reminds us that storytelling is never
only about what is spoken.
It is about what leaks through between the lines.
Your hidden self is always asking to be known.

At the Church of Gnome, we believe every tale is also
confession.
Fiction carries truth.
Exaggeration carries longing.
Silence carries weight.

Listen closely to your own words.
They will show you what remains untended within.
The story you tell is the map of the soul you are still uncovering.

Gnome Blessings.

A joke offered with reverence is a hymn in disguise.

Laughter is not lesser than prayer.
It is another doorway to the sacred.
The smile it brings is its own form of blessing.

This Gnomean Proverb reminds us that joy is holy.
Humor does not trivialize the sacred; it reveals it in softer light.
A heart that can laugh is a heart that has not closed.

At the Church of Gnome, we believe reverence does not mean solemnity alone.
It also means celebration.
It means play.
It means finding holiness in what lifts the spirit as well as what stills it.

Treat laughter as prayer.
Honor it as worship.
For a holy chuckle may heal more than a hundred heavy words.

Gnome Blessings.

Humility lets wisdom in where ego blocked the door.

The proud heart closes itself to learning.
The humble heart opens wide.

This Gnomean Proverb reminds us that wisdom rarely enters
through boasting.
It finds its way through listening.
It enters where there is space, where there is quiet, where there
is room for more than the self.

At the Church of Gnome, we believe humility is not weakness.
It is the soil in which wisdom grows.
Without it, knowledge hardens into arrogance.
With it, knowledge transforms into understanding.

Bow low enough to hear.
Empty yourself enough to receive.
Humility is the door, and wisdom is waiting to walk through.

Gnome Blessings.

In the eyes of the forest, all creatures are equal.

The bird, the fox, the worm, the tree; none is forgotten, none is
exalted above the others.
Each has its place.
Each is part of the whole.

This Gnomean Proverb reminds us that equality is not a human
invention.
It is a truth written into the natural world.
Life honors all its forms, not just the ones we deem grand.

At the Church of Gnome, we believe reverence must extend
beyond our own kind.
The sacred is not partial.
The holy does not play favorites.
Every being, great or small, carries worth.

Walk as though the forest is watching.
Treat each life as though it matters.
For in truth, it does.

Gnome Blessings.

Harmony is not sameness, it is roots growing in different directions, holding the same hill.

Each root takes its own path, twisting and weaving, yet
together they steady the earth.
Unity is not uniformity.
It is strength in diversity.

This Gnomean Proverb reminds us that what holds us together
does not erase our uniqueness.
It honors it.
Difference does not weaken harmony; it completes it.

At the Church of Gnome, we believe belonging is not about
conformity.
It is about interdependence.
We are strongest when our varied roots hold the same ground,
each in its own way.

Do not fear your difference.
It is part of the hill's stability.
Without many roots, there is no harmony at all.

Gnome Blessings.

Guard your peace like a candle in the wind.

It does not take much to disturb it.
One harsh word, one careless gust, and the flame flickers.

This Gnomean Proverb reminds us that peace is not weakness.
It is fragile strength, and it needs protection.
The flame will grow steadier if you shield it, if you choose
carefully where to place it.

At the Church of Gnome, we believe peace is sacred work.
It must be tended, guarded, honored.
Your light matters, and without care, the winds of life will
consume it.

Protect what steadies you.
Defend the flame.
Peace is too holy to leave unguarded.

Gnome Blessings.

A gnome outside the circle often sees the fire most clearly.

Distance sharpens perspective.
From the edge, the whole picture comes into view.

This Gnomean Proverb reminds us that outsiders often hold wisdom insiders miss.
Those who step back or stand apart can notice truths hidden by closeness.
What seems obvious from the margins is often invisible at the center.

At the Church of Gnome, we believe no voice is too far away to matter.
Sometimes the perspective of the one at the edge is the very insight the circle needs.

Honor the center.
Listen to the margin.
The fire is best understood by those who can see both glow and shadow.

Gnome Blessings.

Intuition is your lantern when sight fails.

When the path is unclear, when reason grows dim, when vision falters, the inner flame still glows.

This Gnomean Proverb reminds us that you are not left helpless in the dark.
The lantern is already within you.
It shines in feelings, in knowing without proof, in quiet whispers of the soul.

At the Church of Gnome, we believe intuition is not accident.
It is ancient guidance, a gift to help you walk when logic cannot carry you.
Trust it as you would trust the lantern in your hand.

When sight fails, lift the light within.
It will not lead you astray.

Gnome Blessings.

No words are needed when two hearts breathe together.

Silence becomes its own language.
Presence speaks more than speech ever could.

This Gnomean Proverb reminds us that connection is deeper than language.
Some bonds live beyond vocabulary.
They pulse in rhythm, in closeness, in trust that needs no explanation.

At the Church of Gnome, we believe love is most powerful in its quietest forms.
To share space, to breathe in sync, to simply be together is communion enough.

Do not always reach for words.
Sometimes the silence carries more truth than sound.
Sometimes the shared breath is the prayer.

Gnome Blessings.

Miracles often arrive disguised as repetition.

The sunrise you stop noticing.
The heartbeat you take for granted.
The breath that comes again and again.

This Gnomean Proverb reminds us that the extraordinary hides inside the ordinary.
What looks like routine is often the most profound gift.
Repetition is not dullness.
It is stability, grace, continuity of wonder.

At the Church of Gnome, we believe reverence must be practiced daily.
Miracles are not only the sudden and rare.
They are the steady and constant, the rhythms that keep you alive.

Look again at what repeats.
The miracle has been here all along.

Gnome Blessings.

The salamander dances in flame to remind us fire is not only destruction, but renewal.

What burns is not always lost; it is transformed, clearing the way for what is next.
The fire is dangerous, yes, but also holy in its purging.

This Gnomean Proverb reminds us that change often arrives through heat.
The salamander, guardian of the flame, shows us that endurance is not about resisting fire but learning to move within it.
Destruction and rebirth are two faces of the same blaze.

At the Church of Gnome, we believe fire is a teacher of transformation.
It consumes what can no longer serve, and from its ashes, life begins again.
The salamander's dance is a parable: you cannot fear the flame forever; you must trust what it leaves behind.

Bless the fire for what it clears.
Bless the fire for what it prepares.
The salamander already knows both.

Gnome Blessings.

Resentment is a cage you build around yourself.

It may feel like a weapon, but it only locks you in.
It may feel like protection, but it hardens into prison walls.

This Gnomean Proverb reminds us that resentment punishes
the holder more than the one who caused it.
The bars are real, but they are self-made.
The key is yours to use.

At the Church of Gnome, we believe forgiveness is not approval,
but release.
It is the breaking of chains that no longer serve you.
It is the freedom to breathe outside the cage.

Let go.
Not because they deserve it, but because you do.

Gnome Blessings.

Each lie may shield for a moment, but it stains the lantern glass.

Falsehood can feel like protection, like a quick shelter from danger.
But with each layer, the light dims, and soon even you cannot see your way forward.

This Gnomean Proverb reminds us that lies never disappear; they accumulate.
What begins as convenience becomes obscurity, leaving truth harder and harder to discern.
The shield becomes a prison.

At the Church of Gnome, we believe truth is the clear flame of the lantern.
To guard it is to keep the way visible for yourself and for others.
Every untruth may delay discomfort, but it clouds the very light you rely on to find your path.

Clean the glass.
Speak with honesty.
The lantern was made to shine.

Gnome Blessings.

Gnomes walk with the forest, not through it.

They do not see trees as obstacles or tools.
They see companions, elders, and kin.

This Gnomean Proverb reminds us that the sacred is not
conquered, it is communed with.
To move with the forest is to listen, to honor, to belong.

At the Church of Gnome, we believe the earth is not backdrop,
but partner.
The soil holds memory.
The trees hold wisdom.
The forest holds its own breath of spirit.

Do not trample.
Do not rush.
Walk with, and you will never walk alone.

Gnome Blessings.

Fast grows tall. Slow grows roots.

The quick ascent may impress, but it rarely lasts.
The deeper strength belongs to what took time.

This Gnomean Proverb reminds us that speed is not the same as success.
Growth without grounding is fragile.
Roots unseen are what sustain the visible.

At the Church of Gnome, we believe patience is not delay, but depth.
The slow path is not wasted time.
It is foundation.
It is the unseen strength that steadies you when storms arrive.

Do not envy the quick rise.
Choose the steady rooting.
That is what endures.

Gnome Blessings.

Morning birds are the original prophets.

They announce the new day before the sun confirms it.
Their song is a promise that darkness is never final.

This Gnomean Proverb reminds us that prophecy is not always
thunder or vision.
Sometimes it is as simple as a voice singing into the dark,
trusting that light is on its way.

At the Church of Gnome, we believe wisdom often comes in
small forms.
The birds teach us to welcome the dawn, not with certainty, but
with trust.
They sing not because they see the sun, but because they know
it will come.

Let their chorus remind you: what is unseen can still be
believed.
The light is already on its way.

Gnome Blessings.

A gnome learns more from missteps than shortcuts.

Stumbles teach what smooth paths cannot.
The bruise holds more wisdom than the bypass.

This Gnomean Proverb reminds us that mistakes are not enemies.
They are teachers carved into the journey.
Shortcuts may save time, but they rarely deepen the soul.

At the Church of Gnome, we believe wisdom is written in trial.
Falling, rising, trying again, this is the curriculum of growth.
To avoid difficulty is to avoid depth.

Learn from your missteps.
They will guide you more honestly than the fastest way forward ever could.

Gnome Blessings.

Being unseen is lonely, but also a kind of freedom.

Obscurity aches, but it also shields.
To walk unnoticed can feel like exile, yet it carries its own strange gift.

This Gnomean Proverb reminds us that invisibility is not always absence of worth.
It can be a season of shaping, a place where roots grow in hidden strength.

At the Church of Gnome, we believe freedom sometimes wears the cloak of loneliness.
What feels like neglect may actually be protection.
What feels like silence may actually be space.

Do not despise the hidden seasons.
They prepare you for what comes next.
And in them, you may find a freedom too deep for the crowd to offer.

Gnome Blessings.

The tongue that cuts another's craft often bleeds with its own unfinished work.

Criticism sharpens quickest when turned outward to mask inner fear.
What is mocked in another is often what is unhealed within.

This Gnomean Proverb reminds us that tearing down is easier than building.
But every cut carries the echo of the cutter's own wounds.

At the Church of Gnome, we believe creation deserves reverence.
Even the imperfect work of another is sacred in its attempt.
To cut it cruelly is to reveal your own hidden struggle.

If you must speak, let your words water, not wither.
For your own craft is listening, and it will reflect the voice you use.

Gnome Blessings.

Choose what brings peace, not just applause.

The crowd will cheer what dazzles.
But only your soul knows what sustains.

This Gnomean Proverb reminds us that applause fades quickly,
while peace endures.
The sound of approval cannot quiet the unrest of a divided
spirit.
Only alignment with your truth can do that.

At the Church of Gnome, we believe peace is the truest measure
of success.
Fame may come and go.
Acclaim may rise and fall.
But peace, once chosen, becomes an anchor.

Seek what steadies you, not only what pleases others.
Choose the quieter reward.
It is the only one that lasts.

Gnome Blessings.

When stories feed only on sorrow, they starve the soul of hope.

Grief has its place, but when it becomes the only tale told, it closes the door to renewal.
A life remembered only by pain forgets its own light.

This Gnomean Proverb reminds us that sorrow must be honored, but it must also be balanced.
Hope is not denial of loss.
It is the thread that allows sorrow to transform into meaning.

At the Church of Gnome, we believe every story carries both ache and beauty.
To tell one without the other is to give only half the truth.
Let grief speak, but let hope speak also.

Your story is not only what hurt.
It is also what healed, what endured, what blossomed in the cracks.

Gnome Blessings.

Light that refuses to touch shadow is just decoration.

It shines for appearance, not for purpose.
It glitters, but it does not guide.

This Gnomean Proverb reminds us that true light is brave.
It enters what is hidden.
It softens what is hard.
It offers warmth where cold once claimed dominion.

At the Church of Gnome, we believe the sacred task of light is
not to avoid the dark, but to transform it.
Illumination is not for spectacle, but for healing.
It matters because it reaches where it is needed most.

Do not settle for display.
Be light that dares to enter the shadow.

Gnome Blessings.

Let your voice carry what your heart holds.

Unspoken truths weigh heavy.
Silent love can wither unshared.
The heart is not meant to remain a locked chamber.

This Gnomean Proverb reminds us that words are vessels.
They give form to feeling.
They release what would otherwise remain buried.

At the Church of Gnome, we believe speech is sacred when it
rises from the heart.
It becomes a bridge, turning solitude into connection, turning
silence into presence.

Let your words be honest.
Let them reveal rather than conceal.
When your voice carries what your heart holds, healing begins.

Gnome Blessings.

To walk barefoot is to return to the original altar.

The soil, the stone, the grass beneath your feet are the first holy ground.
Before temples and scriptures, there was earth.

This Gnomean Proverb reminds us that contact with the ground is contact with the sacred.
It draws you back to humility, back to belonging, back to the truth that you are not separate from the world.

At the Church of Gnome, we believe reverence begins underfoot.
Every step barefoot is prayer.
Every touch of skin to soil is communion.

Remove the barrier.
Let the earth remind you who you are.
Let the altar hold you with each step.

Gnome Blessings.

A beard may grow long, but discernment grows only with listening.

Time alone does not make wisdom.
Years can pass, hair can lengthen, but without openness, the spirit remains shallow.

This Gnomean Proverb reminds us that appearance and age are not proof of insight.
Wisdom is cultivated not in the mirror, but in the ear; in the willingness to hear, to learn, to consider.

At the Church of Gnome, we believe wisdom requires humility.
It is less about how long you have lived and more about how deeply you have listened.
Every person carries a story; to honor it is to let it shape your own.

Do not measure wisdom by beard or years.
Measure it by how often you listen, and how fully you let yourself be changed.

Gnome Blessings.

Love without ownership is the gnome way.

Affection is not possession.
To hold someone does not mean to hold them captive.
Love thrives in freedom, not in control.

This Gnomean Proverb reminds us that love is most sacred
when it is given, not grasped.
It is the open hand, not the closed fist.
It grows strongest when it allows space for the beloved to
remain themselves.

At the Church of Gnome, we believe true love is companionship,
not captivity.
It honors the other as whole, as free, as equal.
It is covenant, not contract.

Love them without chains.
Love them without fear.
Love them so they can stand beside you, not beneath you.

Gnome Blessings.

What was forced is not sacred.

The holy cannot be taken by demand.
It cannot be shaped by coercion.
It withers when stripped of freedom.

This Gnomean Proverb reminds us that the sacred rests in consent, in choice, in authenticity.
Anything pressed by fear or pressure may look holy, but it carries no spirit within.

At the Church of Gnome, we believe what is real must be chosen.
Faith must be lived, not imposed.
Love must be offered, not seized.
Sacredness cannot be forced into being; it must arrive through freedom.

Let what is true emerge willingly.
That is where the sacred dwells.

Gnome Blessings.

Release your grip on their past, if you want to meet their present.

You cannot embrace who they are now if your arms are still wrapped around who they were.
The past may explain them, but it does not define them.

This Gnomean Proverb reminds us that love requires letting go of outdated versions of one another.
To cling to the old story is to miss the new one unfolding.

At the Church of Gnome, we believe every soul is a river, moving and reshaping itself constantly.
Respecting someone means walking with their current, not chaining them to their banks.

Loosen your hold.
Look again with fresh eyes.
The one you love is here now, waiting to be seen.

Gnome Blessings.

The shadow you refuse to meet grows larger behind you.

Avoidance does not dissolve it.
Denial does not weaken it.
What is ignored only gathers strength in silence.

This Gnomean Proverb reminds us that courage is not running
from darkness, but turning to face it.
To meet your shadow is to shrink it.
To deny it is to let it grow unchecked.

At the Church of Gnome, we believe healing requires
confrontation.
Wholeness is found not in light alone, but in the union of light
with what it illuminates.
Your shadow is not your enemy.
It is your unacknowledged teacher.

Face it.
Name it.
Only then will it lose its hold.

Gnome Blessings.

The deeper the love, the quieter the world feels without them.

Absence echoes loudest where love once lived most deeply.
The silence becomes its own presence, heavy with memory.

This Gnomean Proverb reminds us that grief is not proof of
weakness.
It is proof of devotion.
The quiet after their departure is not emptiness; it is love
transformed into longing.

At the Church of Gnome, we believe grief is sacred.
It is the shadow of love, inseparable from it.
To mourn deeply is to honor the depth of the bond that was
shared.

Do not fear the quiet.
Sit with it gently.
It is filled with the sound of love that refuses to end.

Gnome Blessings.

What you call strange may simply be sacred in a dialect you forgot.

The unfamiliar often feels unsettling.
The mysterious can appear foolish or wrong to the one who has forgotten its language.

This Gnomean Proverb reminds us that mystery wears many forms.
What is foreign to you may be holy to another.
What you dismiss may actually be an echo of something your soul once knew.

At the Church of Gnome, we believe reverence includes honoring what feels strange.
Sacredness does not depend on our comfort.
It lives beyond our understanding, waiting for us to remember.

Treat the unfamiliar gently.
It may not be nonsense.
It may be memory calling you back to wonder.

Gnome Blessings.

When the river of justice dries, the dust of cruelty spreads.

Where fairness is withheld, resentment festers.
Where dignity is denied, violence rises like storm.

This Gnomean Proverb reminds us that justice is not a luxury,
but the water that sustains peace.
Without it, the ground cracks and dust takes the air, choking
the very life it once nourished.

At the Church of Gnome, we believe justice is sacred
stewardship.
It is the tending of the river that keeps cruelty from filling the
land.
When the river flows, life thrives along its banks.
When it dries, shadows multiply.

Guard the river.
Keep it flowing.
For all who thirst, justice is the water of life.

Gnome Blessings.

To be fully seen is to risk being fully loved.

Exposure is frightening.
Vulnerability feels dangerous.
But it is also the doorway to the love that cannot live behind walls.

This Gnomean Proverb reminds us that love cannot thrive in half-truths.
It needs the whole of you; the tender, the flawed, the beautiful, the unguarded.
To be seen fully is to be known, and to be known is the only way to be truly loved.

At the Church of Gnome, we believe love requires courage.
The risk of being seen is the price of the gift.
And the gift is worth it.

Step into the light.
Love is waiting.

Gnome Blessings.

Anchor peace in your body, and your mind will follow.

Breathe slowly.
Rest your shoulders.
Let the tension release.
The mind learns calm by following the body's lead.

This Gnomean Proverb reminds us that peace is not only an idea.
It is physical.
It is felt in rhythm, in breath, in the grounding of the body.

At the Church of Gnome, we believe the body is not separate from the spirit.
To steady the body is to steady the soul.
To tend the body is to invite the mind back into balance.

Begin with breath.
Begin with rest.
Peace will come as the body teaches the mind to return home.

Gnome Blessings.

Happiness multiplies when carried together.

Joy shared is not divided; it expands, weaving itself between hearts, doubling its strength with each connection.
The laughter of one is sweet, but the laughter of many becomes song.

This Gnomean Proverb reminds us that joy is not meant to be hoarded.
It is not treasure locked away, but light that grows stronger when reflected.
When happiness is shared, it ceases to be fragile; it becomes resilient.

At the Church of Gnome, we believe happiness is communal by nature.
We were not designed to rejoice alone, but to magnify joy in the presence of others.
It is in sharing that happiness becomes durable, enduring far beyond the moment.

Do not hold your joy in silence.
Offer it freely.
See how it multiplies.

Gnome Blessings.

Moss welcomes all feet without question.

It does not measure worth.
It does not choose which step is worthy of rest.
It simply offers softness to whoever walks upon it.

This Gnomean Proverb reminds us that belonging can be as
simple as welcome.
True hospitality asks for nothing in return.
It honors the traveler as they are, weary or whole.

At the Church of Gnome, we believe love should be like moss.
Open, steady, unconditional.
To welcome without judgment is to mirror the sacred.

Be moss for others.
Let your presence be the softness that carries them forward.

Gnome Blessings.

No moment is truly wasted if you wake in the next one.

Regret does not erase time, but awareness transforms it.
The moment missed becomes the moment found if you choose
to return to presence.

This Gnomean Proverb reminds us that mistakes are not final
verdicts.
Every breath is a chance to begin again.
Every heartbeat is an invitation back to now.

At the Church of Gnome, we believe presence redeems the past.
Awakening in the next moment is enough.
You are not condemned to what has passed; you are invited to
what remains.

Wake again.
Begin again.
The gift is still here.

Gnome Blessings.

Peace is not always in the answer, but in the asking.

The question itself can hold calm.
The curiosity itself can be prayer.

This Gnomean Proverb reminds us that certainty is not required for serenity.
Sometimes the peace comes from letting the question live without rushing to solve it.
Sometimes wonder is its own kind of rest.

At the Church of Gnome, we believe seeking is as holy as finding.
The question has beauty of its own.
The asking is a doorway into trust.

Do not fear unanswered questions.
They may already be carrying the peace you long for.

Gnome Blessings.

Inner truth doesn't compete to be heard.

It does not shout or demand.
It waits, quiet, steady, patient.

This Gnomean Proverb reminds us that wisdom within is not frantic.
It is gentle.
It will not force its way against the noise of the world.
But if you still yourself, it will speak.

At the Church of Gnome, we believe the inner voice is the lantern of the soul.
It may flicker softly, but it never goes out.
To hear it, you need only make space.

Turn down the noise.
Trust the whisper.
Your truth is waiting.

Gnome Blessings.

Refusing to change is itself a kind of transformation.

Even stillness shifts you.
Even resistance shapes you.
To deny movement is still to be moved, only in ways unseen.

This Gnomean Proverb reminds us that transformation is inevitable.
It does not depend on our permission.
Even when we cling to sameness, change continues its work beneath the surface.

At the Church of Gnome, we believe every choice, even refusal, carries weight.
To resist growth is still to be altered by the passage of time.
To fight change is still to be changed by the fight itself.

You cannot escape transformation.
But you can choose whether it bends you toward openness or hardens you against it.

Gnome Blessings.

The wind does not belong to the flute.

The song is not owned by the instrument.
It is carried through, borrowed for a moment, then released.

This Gnomean Proverb reminds us that what flows through us
is not ours to keep.
Gifts, talents, wisdom; they are not possessions.
They are visitations, moving through us to reach others.

At the Church of Gnome, we believe life itself is borrowed
breath.
To receive is holy, but so is the letting go.
To be a vessel is to honor what was never yours to claim.

Do not cling to the wind.
Let it pass through.
The music remains because it was shared.

Gnome Blessings.

The sacred hides in the crack, not the cathedral.

It seeps through broken walls, through overlooked spaces, through what seems unworthy of reverence.

This Gnomean Proverb reminds us that holiness often dwells in what is small and fractured.
Not in grandeur alone, but in what humbles and softens.
Not in perfect design, but in the places life slips quietly through.

At the Church of Gnome, we believe the sacred refuses to be caged by walls or monuments.
It lives where vulnerability opens.
It shines where imperfection lets the light enter.

Look not only to the towering halls.
Look to the cracks.
That is where wonder waits.

Gnome Blessings.

The more you try to define the sacred, the more it escapes into your periphery.

The moment you draw hard lines around it, it slips past the frame, spilling into the edges you were too rigid to see.
The sacred was never meant to be contained; it was meant to be encountered.

This Gnomean Proverb reminds us that the divine resists confinement.
Creeds, doctrines, and definitions can point toward mystery, but they cannot replace it.
The holy remains larger than the names we give it, moving always beyond capture.

At the Church of Gnome, we believe reverence lives not in mastery but in humility.
The sacred is present in the things we cannot measure, in the silences that cannot be filled, in the wonder that persists no matter how many words we stack upon it.

Look not only at the center of your vision.
Pay attention to the periphery, to the shimmer at the edges of your knowing.
That is where the sacred waits to be seen.

Gnome Blessings.

A single honest word can outweigh a thousand spoken for noise.

Clamor may fill the air, but only truth carries weight that lasts.
Noise passes quickly; honesty plants itself deeply.

This Gnomean Proverb reminds us that words are not measured
by quantity, but by substance.
The simplest truth spoken with sincerity can change more than
endless chatter.
One seed of truth can grow into a forest, while countless empty
words scatter like dust.

At the Church of Gnome, we believe honesty is sacred speech.
To speak with clarity is to shine light where shadows would
linger.
The tongue is most powerful when it chooses truth over
volume.

Speak less, if you must, but speak true.
The weight of honesty will always endure.

Gnome Blessings.

Even a lantern dims when never tended.

Neglect, not just storms, causes the flame to fade.
Every light requires care to keep burning.

This Gnomean Proverb reminds us that your inner fire is not
self-sustaining.
It needs attention.
It needs renewal.
It needs your willingness to guard it against exhaustion.

At the Church of Gnome, we believe tending the spirit is daily
practice.
Rest, reflection, gratitude; these are the oil that keep the
lantern alive.

Do not abandon your own flame.
Tend it.
Feed it.
Let it shine with the strength it was meant to carry.

Gnome Blessings.

They ask for food, but give you yourself.

A pet's hunger may bring them near, but what they offer in
return is far greater.
Their loyalty mirrors your worth.
Their presence calls forth your gentleness.
Their trust awakens your own humanity.

This Gnomean Proverb reminds us that pets are not only
companions of comfort, but of reflection.
They reveal the parts of us that are tender, patient, and kind.
In feeding them, we are reminded of the nourishment we are
capable of giving.

At the Church of Gnome, we believe animals are sacred
companions.
Their gift is not measured in words, but in presence.
They show us who we are when we are at our most honest.

Feed them well.
For in doing so, you are feeding what is best within yourself.

Gnome Blessings.

Hiding your oddness is like burying a lantern.

The very thing that makes you shine becomes lost beneath the soil.
The world grows darker when you hide what was meant to give light.

This Gnomean Proverb reminds us that uniqueness is not flaw, but fire.
It is your strangeness that illuminates paths others could not see.
To bury it is to rob the world of needed brightness.

At the Church of Gnome, we believe authenticity is sacred.
The oddness you fear is often the very gift another has been waiting for.
Let it be seen.
Let it glow.

Your lantern was not meant for the ground.
It was meant for the night.

Gnome Blessings.

Certainty is the heaviest thing a fool can carry.

It drags the spirit down, closing it off from wonder, from
learning, from change.
The more tightly it is held, the less room there is for truth to
enter.

This Gnomean Proverb reminds us that wisdom requires
openness.
To be too sure is to be blind.
To admit you do not know is to begin to see.

At the Church of Gnome, we believe humility is lighter than
pride.
It frees you to grow, to listen, to discover.
Certainty locks the door.
Curiosity leaves it open.

Lay down the burden of needing to be right.
Carry instead the freedom of seeking.

Gnome Blessings.

The landvættir guard respect more fiercely than territory.

They do not count acres or draw borders, for the earth does not belong to us.
What they protect is reverence; whether we approach the land with humility or with greed.

This Gnomean Proverb reminds us that the sacred is not threatened by our presence, but by our posture.
To step lightly is to walk as guest.
To plunder is to forget that the ground itself is alive and watching.

At the Church of Gnome, we believe land is not possession but relationship.
The landvættir do not measure your worth by what you take, but by how you bow, how you tend, how you honor what you stand upon.

Tread with care.
Offer your respect before you ask for the land's gifts.
The guardians are listening.

Gnome Blessings.

Trust returns like moss to stone; slow, quiet, but steadfast if given light and time.

At first the surface looks bare, stripped of what once grew.
But patience restores what was lost.
Tenderness brings life back again.

This Gnomean Proverb reminds us that trust cannot be forced.
It does not return by demand.
It grows naturally, and only with care.

At the Church of Gnome, we believe forgiveness is not always instant, but it is always possible.
Time and gentleness can cover even the hardest surfaces with new life.
What seems barren can become green again.

Do not rush the moss.
Let it grow in its own time.
When trust returns, it will be steady.

Gnome Blessings.

Reflection turns fire into light.

Anger without pause destroys.
But when considered, when softened, when understood, it
becomes illumination.

This Gnomean Proverb reminds us that intensity alone is not
wisdom.
The flame must be transformed through reflection to guide
rather than scorch.

At the Church of Gnome, we believe every fire within us carries
the potential for vision.
When reflected upon, it reveals truth, clarity, and even
compassion.
When left unchecked, it consumes without purpose.

Do not fear your fire.
Reflect upon it until it becomes light for your path.

Gnome Blessings.

Intentional silence is a spell of restoration.

In the quiet, the spirit resets.
In the stillness, the body gathers strength again.

This Gnomean Proverb reminds us that silence is not absence.
It is presence of a deeper kind.
It heals, restores, and balances what noise has frayed.

At the Church of Gnome, we believe silence is sacred practice.
It is medicine for the soul.
It is the pause that makes all other sounds meaningful.

Choose silence sometimes.
It will return to you as peace.

Gnome Blessings.

What walls cannot break, love walks through as if they were air.

Force meets resistance, but love finds passage where no opening was thought to exist.
It does not batter; it permeates.
It does not demand; it transforms.

This Gnomean Proverb reminds us that love is not bound by barriers.
Its strength is not in violence, but in persistence, in patience, in the way it moves quietly through every crack and opening.
Walls cannot contain what was born to flow.

At the Church of Gnome, we believe love is the most enduring force in existence.
Where anger hardens, love softens.
Where cruelty closes, love finds entry.
No fortress is strong enough to withstand it forever.

Do not despair at the wall.
Love has already passed through.

Gnome Blessings.

Every true ritual is a doorway, not a performance.

It is not crafted for applause, nor meant to impress.
Its purpose is not to entertain; it is to transform.

This Gnomean Proverb reminds us that ritual, at its heart, is a threshold.
It ushers you from one state of being to another.
The gestures may be simple, the words few, but if done with reverence, the veil thins and you find yourself standing in a different world.

At the Church of Gnome, we believe ritual becomes holy when it is sincere.
Without heart, it is empty.
With presence, it becomes an opening into mystery.
Every ritual, no matter how small, is an invitation to cross over.

Do not perform your prayers.
Walk through them.
The sacred is waiting on the other side of the doorway.

Gnome Blessings.

The stomach knows when the soul is shouting.

The body feels what the spirit carries long before the mind
admits it.
Restlessness, tension, unease; they are the language of the
inner self.

This Gnomean Proverb reminds us that the body is not separate
from the soul.
It reveals what you cannot yet say aloud.
It calls for attention, for care, for honesty.

At the Church of Gnome, we believe the sacred voice of intuition
often speaks through the body.
To ignore it is to turn from truth.
To honor it is to walk in alignment with your own being.

Listen to your stomach.
It is the soul speaking in flesh and feeling.

Gnome Blessings.

Let your heart be light, and your roots be deep.

Carry joy easily, but hold your ground firmly.
A life without weight drifts.
A life without depth topples.

This Gnomean Proverb reminds us that balance is sacred.
The heart was made for laughter, wonder, and trust.
The roots were made for steadiness, resilience, and endurance.
Together they form a wholeness the world cannot shake.

At the Church of Gnome, we believe true wisdom is not
choosing one or the other.
It is the marriage of both.
To dance lightly while rooted deeply is the way of peace.

Gnome Blessings.

The peace you grow becomes shelter for those near.

Your calm steadies more than your own soul.
It offers refuge to all who come close.

This Gnomean Proverb reminds us that inner work is never
only for ourselves.
The serenity you cultivate ripples outward, becoming
protection, becoming shade, becoming home for others.

At the Church of Gnome, we believe peace is contagious.
One heart at rest softens many.
One life grounded becomes shelter for weary ones nearby.

Grow your peace like a tree.
Its branches will hold more than you know.

Gnome Blessings.

The sylph reminds us that every breath is borrowed sky.

Invisible, intangible, yet essential; air moves through us as gift,
never as possession.
Each inhale is a reminder that life is not earned but received.

This Gnomean Proverb reminds us that we are woven into the
atmosphere, sustained by what cannot be held in our hands.
To breathe is to participate in a cycle older than humanity
itself, a covenant of exchange between body and world.

At the Church of Gnome, we believe reverence begins with
breath.
The sylph is the whispering spirit of the wind, reminding us
that every exhale returns what was never ours to keep.
To breathe with awareness is to pray without words.

Do not take the air for granted.
Borrow it gratefully.
Return it gently.

Gnome Blessings.

Gnomes know; if it makes no sense, it might be sacred.

The rational mind is not the only path to truth.
Wonder, paradox, and strangeness often carry wisdom too
large for logic.

This Gnomean Proverb reminds us that the sacred does not
always bow to reason.
It dances, it confuses, it unsettles, and in that space, it
transforms.

At the Church of Gnome, we believe mystery is not to be solved,
but honored.
Nonsense may be revelation in disguise.
Confusion may be the threshold of deeper sight.

Do not reject what you cannot explain.
Hold it gently.
Let it speak in its own way.

Gnome Blessings.

If you hold someone's grief gently, your own may find rest.

Compassion is not only for the other.
It heals the giver too.
Shared sorrow softens both hearts at once.

This Gnomean Proverb reminds us that empathy is a mirror.
When you comfort another, you touch the part of yourself still aching.
When you hold their pain with care, your own begins to breathe again.

At the Church of Gnome, we believe grief is never meant to be carried alone.
When we bear one another's sorrow, it loses some of its weight.
When we listen, when we cradle, when we honor, healing quietly begins.

Hold another's grief with tenderness.
In doing so, you may finally cradle your own.

Gnome Blessings.

Some truths were planted by fear, not wisdom.

They were sown to control, to protect, to limit.
They masquerade as certainty, but they were never rooted in love.

This Gnomean Proverb reminds us that not all lessons deserve to endure.
What you were taught as truth may be nothing more than fear given a voice.
The soil of fear grows walls, not freedom.

At the Church of Gnome, we believe wisdom is measured by the fruit it bears.
If it nurtures peace, kindness, and courage, it is truth.
If it binds you in shame, it is fear wearing holy clothes.

Examine the roots.
Keep what brings life.
Release what was only planted to keep you small.

Gnome Blessings.

Not knowing is not danger, it's the beginning of wonder.

Uncertainty does not mean failure.
It is the space where awe begins, where possibility grows.

This Gnomean Proverb reminds us that questions are not threats.
They are invitations.
They open paths that answers alone cannot create.

At the Church of Gnome, we believe mystery is not the absence of knowledge, but the presence of something greater than knowledge.
Wonder begins where certainty ends.
Unknowing is not emptiness; it is fertile ground.

Trust your questions.
They may lead you further than answers ever could.

Gnome Blessings.

Even gnomes lose their hats to storms and bless the wind for it.

Loss can feel humiliating, stripping us of what we thought defined us.
But sometimes what is taken clears the way for something better.

This Gnomean Proverb reminds us that storms do not only break.
They also cleanse.
They strip away what you clung to so tightly, so you can discover you are more than what you wore.

At the Church of Gnome, we believe resilience is not just surviving the storm, but finding gratitude within it.
To bless the wind is to honor its role in revealing your deeper strength.

Do not curse what was lost.
See what remains.
Bless the storm for reminding you who you are without the hat.

Gnome Blessings.

The longer you avoid your truth, the more it leaks through your actions.

What is hidden will still find its way out.
Silence and denial cannot hold forever.

This Gnomean Proverb reminds us that truth has endurance.
It will press through in tone, in choices, in unspoken words,
until it is finally faced.

At the Church of Gnome, we believe honesty with yourself is the
foundation of freedom.
To bury truth is to exhaust yourself with constant leakage.
To embrace truth is to release the burden and live in alignment.

Face it.
Name it.
Let it free you rather than haunt you.

Gnome Blessings.

Self-forgiveness is not forgetting, it's finally understanding.

It does not erase what happened.
It sees it fully, with clarity and compassion, and chooses to hold yourself gently anyway.

This Gnomean Proverb reminds us that forgiveness is not denial.
It is transformation.
It shifts blame into wisdom, pain into tenderness, error into growth.

At the Church of Gnome, we believe forgiving yourself is an act of courage.
It is not dismissal of your past, but a new relationship with it.
One where you are no longer enemy to yourself.

Understand what shaped you.
Honor the lessons.
And choose to walk forward in peace.

Gnome Blessings.

A gnome once whispered, "We're here to garden the mystery, not solve it."

Life is not a puzzle to be conquered, but a field to be tended.
Mystery is not meant to be undone, but cultivated with reverence.

This Gnomean Proverb reminds us that wisdom is not found in certainty, but in care.
The sacred grows when we water it with wonder, when we let it flourish without demanding control.

At the Church of Gnome, we believe mystery is the soil of meaning.
To tend it is to live faithfully.
To solve it is to miss its gift.

Garden gently.
Let the unknown bloom.
It was never meant to be harvested, only honored.

Gnome Blessings.

Let the ashes rest. You've already gathered enough from that fire.

The lesson has been learned.
The loss has been felt.
To keep sifting only covers you in soot again.

This Gnomean Proverb reminds us that healing requires release.
There comes a time when returning to the remains keeps you from moving into what's ahead.

At the Church of Gnome, we believe wisdom is carried, not clutched.
The fire gave its teaching.
The ashes do not need to be your dwelling.

Lay them down.
Carry only the warmth of what was given.
Leave the soot where it belongs.

Gnome Blessings.

The wiser the being, the lower they sit.

Pride rises, but wisdom descends.
It finds its place in humility, in listening, in stillness near the ground.

This Gnomean Proverb reminds us that wisdom is not shown in height, but in depth.
The loud may demand attention, but the humble carry true strength.

At the Church of Gnome, we believe wisdom is always close to the soil.
It chooses humility over throne, service over spectacle.
To sit low is to see clearly.

Lower yourself.
There is more truth near the ground than in any lofty perch.

Gnome Blessings.

Criticism without curiosity is hollow noise.

To judge without asking is to shout into emptiness.
It creates nothing, teaches nothing, heals nothing.

This Gnomean Proverb reminds us that curiosity is what
transforms critique into wisdom.
Questions open the door.
Assumptions close it.

At the Church of Gnome, we believe discernment is sacred, but
cruelty is not.
A question honors another's humanity.
Condemnation without seeking only dishonors yourself.

Before you speak against, ask.
Without curiosity, your words are only clamor.

Gnome Blessings.

In every myth, there's a memory.

Stories carry the trace of what once was.
Legends hold fragments of truth woven with imagination.

This Gnomean Proverb reminds us that myths are not only
fantasy.
They are vessels of memory, preserving wisdom, history, and
longing.
They are the way ancestors speak to us across time.

At the Church of Gnome, we believe myth is sacred language.
It remembers what the world has forgotten.
It keeps alive what history could not hold in fact alone.

Listen to the myth.
Search for the memory within it.
There you will find the roots of truth.

Gnome Blessings.

Even a mushroom cracks concrete in time.

What seems fragile carries its own power.
Patience is its strength, persistence its teacher.

This Gnomean Proverb reminds us that gentleness is not weakness.
What grows slowly can still overturn what looks unbreakable.
The soft will always outlast the rigid.

At the Church of Gnome, we believe resilience wears many forms.
It is not only force, but endurance.
It is not only speed, but constancy.

Trust the mushroom.
Its quiet persistence reshapes even stone.

Gnome Blessings.

One spark of kindness silences more shadows than a lifetime of complaint.

Darkness does not yield to curses.
It retreats in the presence of even the smallest light.

This Gnomean Proverb reminds us that negativity may reveal
the problem, but kindness creates the solution.
A complaint without compassion changes little; a single act of
care changes everything.

At the Church of Gnome, we believe kindness is sacred fire.
It does not need to be large to matter.
Even one spark shifts the atmosphere, driving away what
despair tried to claim.

When you are tempted to curse the shadows, pause.
Choose instead to light a spark.
That is how the night begins to fade.

Gnome Blessings.

Nature doesn't need our guilt. It needs our hands.

Shame will not heal the river.
Regret will not regrow the forest.
Only action restores what has been harmed.

This Gnomean Proverb reminds us that love for the earth must
become labor.
Feelings without deeds are only half the offering.

At the Church of Gnome, we believe stewardship is sacred
responsibility.
To care for the earth is not punishment; it is devotion.
It is gratitude made visible in action.

Put your hands to the soil.
Let your love be work.
That is how healing begins.

Gnome Blessings.

Those who silence dialogue reveal the weakness of their cause.

Truth does not fear questions.
Wisdom does not hide from conversation.
Only falsehood trembles at the sound of another voice.

This Gnomean Proverb reminds us that strength is shown not in suppression, but in openness.
The cause that cannot withstand dialogue is already fragile.
To close ears is to confess fear of exposure.

At the Church of Gnome, we believe dialogue is sacred exchange.
Even disagreement can sharpen, refine, and reveal deeper truth.
To silence it is to cut off the very air that wisdom breathes.

Do not fear the question.
Invite it.
What is true will only shine brighter when spoken aloud.

Gnome Blessings.

A crooked line drawn in truth sings louder than a straight one drawn in fear.

Perfection without honesty is hollow.
Flaws born of sincerity carry more beauty than flawless falsehood.

This Gnomean Proverb reminds us that integrity matters more than image.
The trembling hand that draws truth is stronger than the steady hand that draws a lie.

At the Church of Gnome, we believe authenticity is sacred.
It is better to walk imperfectly in honesty than to walk flawlessly in fear.
The song of truth always rings louder, no matter the shape it takes.

Choose the crooked line if it is true.
It will always shine brighter than fear's perfection.

Gnome Blessings.

The moon gathers what the sun left scattered.

Daylight runs wild, filling the world with motion and distraction.
But in the hush of night, the moon gathers it all, weaving clarity from chaos, silence from noise.

This Gnomean Proverb reminds us that reflection often follows activity.
The lessons of the day are not always learned in the moment, but in the stillness afterward.
The moon teaches us to pause, to collect, to see what was overlooked.

At the Church of Gnome, we believe the rhythms of light and dark mirror the rhythms of the soul.
We need both the scattering of action and the gathering of reflection.
The sacred waits in the balance between them.

Let the sun scatter.
Let the moon gather.
Both belong to you.

Gnome Blessings.

Roots may twist in different directions, yet all trees drink from the same rain.

Difference is not division.
Diversity is not disconnection.

This Gnomean Proverb reminds us that beneath all variations of belief, culture, and life, there is shared nourishment.
We all drink from the same sky.
We are all sustained by the same gift.

At the Church of Gnome, we believe unity does not erase uniqueness.
It honors it.
It celebrates that difference and connection can live side by side.

Twist in your own direction.
Drink deeply of the same rain.
Belong to the same whole.

Gnome Blessings.

To break a pattern is to bless those who come after you.

Cycles of harm do not end on their own.
It takes one person's courage to interrupt what has always been.

This Gnomean Proverb reminds us that healing is generational.
When you refuse to repeat what hurt you, you create space for new life.
Your choice becomes inheritance.

At the Church of Gnome, we believe bravery is not only for yourself.
It is for those you may never meet, those who will live freer because of what you ended.

Break what needs breaking.
The blessing will echo forward.

Gnome Blessings.

A kind word plants roots in places you may never walk.

The soil of another's heart may hold your blessing long after you have forgotten the moment.
What feels small to you may grow into shelter for someone far down their path.

This Gnomean Proverb reminds us that kindness is not measured by immediacy.
Its fruit may ripen where you never see, and its roots may strengthen lives you never meet.
The impact is not lost simply because it is hidden.

At the Church of Gnome, we believe words are seeds.
Every encouragement, every blessing, every honest kindness has a future beyond your vision.
To speak them is to sow into the mystery.

Speak anyway.
Plant anyway.
The garden will grow, even if your eyes never see it.

Gnome Blessings.

Avoidance dressed in productivity still leaves the roots untended.

You can fill your days with tasks and still miss the work that
matters.
Busyness is not the same as growth.

This Gnomean Proverb reminds us that distraction often
masquerades as diligence.
But the roots will still wither if left ignored.
True tending requires depth, not just activity.

At the Church of Gnome, we believe sacred labor is not
measured by quantity, but by alignment.
Better to touch the root once with care than to cover the surface
endlessly.

Do not confuse motion with meaning.
Return to the roots.
That is where life is sustained.

Gnome Blessings.

Some teachers wag their tails and never speak a word.

Their lessons are presence, loyalty, and joy.
They do not lecture, yet their wisdom runs deep.

This Gnomean Proverb reminds us that not all guidance comes from books or voices.
Sometimes it comes on four legs, with fur, with eyes that see straight into your spirit.

At the Church of Gnome, we believe animals carry truths we forget.
They remind us of simplicity, of love without condition, of joy in the smallest things.

Honor these teachers.
Learn from them.
Their silence is wisdom, their presence a blessing.

Gnome Blessings.

Condemn deeds if you must, but never mistake a human life for waste.

You may disagree deeply with someone's choices, words, or beliefs.
You may find their actions misguided, even harmful to the harmony you value.
But their life itself remains sacred.

This Gnomean Proverb reminds us that people are more than the opinions they carry or the mistakes they make in expression.
To reduce them to a single deed or viewpoint is to miss the complexity of their humanity.
We can reject ideas without erasing the worth of the person who holds them.

At the Church of Gnome, we believe disagreement is part of life's fabric.
It sharpens us, challenges us, and sometimes frustrates us.
But even across divides, the truth remains: every life carries the same spark of dignity, the same thread of mystery, the same unshakable worth.

Speak honestly against what you cannot support.
Hold firm to your values.
But do not let contempt convince you that another soul is disposable.
To honor life, even in difference, is to keep your own lantern lit.

Gnome Blessings.

Modern life needs ancient rhythm.

The clocks spin faster, the screens glow brighter, but the body still longs for sunrise and sunset, for planting and harvest, for rest and return.

This Gnomean Proverb reminds us that technology cannot erase our oldest truths.
The spirit is not nourished by constant speed.
It is nourished by cycles, pauses, and seasons.

At the Church of Gnome, we believe to be human is to remember the old ways.
To honor sleep, food, earth, and community.
To let your soul breathe in rhythm with the eternal patterns of nature.

Slow down.
Return to rhythm.
Life will meet you there.

Gnome Blessings.

If they exile you for truth, build a temple from the stones they threw.

Rejection can become foundation.
Condemnation can become sanctuary.

This Gnomean Proverb reminds us that persecution does not end the sacred; it often strengthens it.
The very force that tried to destroy you may become the material of your resilience.

At the Church of Gnome, we believe exile is not the end of belonging.
It is the birthplace of new community.
Every stone cast in hatred can be turned into a pillar of hope.

Do not curse the stones.
Build with them.
Let your temple rise from what was meant to bury you.

Gnome Blessings.

A mouth that delights in whispers never stays loyal to one ear.

The tongue that gossips does not discriminate; it wounds whoever is near.
What it betrays for you, it will betray of you.

This Gnomean Proverb reminds us that secrecy spoken in malice corrodes trust.
What begins as curiosity or amusement quickly becomes poison, spreading further than intended.
The whisperer is not ally, but liability.

At the Church of Gnome, we believe words are sacred tools, meant to build, not to betray.
To delight in gossip is to dim the lantern of your own character.
Better to keep silence than to spread a shadow with your speech.

Do not feed the whisper.
It will not remain in your favor.

Gnome Blessings.

You are not alone. You are simply in the company of your own becoming.

Loneliness may feel like emptiness, but often it is the quiet space where transformation is unfolding.
The self you are meeting needs room to grow.

This Gnomean Proverb reminds us that solitude can be sacred.
It is not the absence of connection, but the presence of your own unfolding.

At the Church of Gnome, we believe becoming requires time with yourself.
This is not exile; it is initiation.
The person you are becoming is arriving to meet you.

Sit gently with your own company.
It may be the most important companionship of all.

Gnome Blessings.

The birds sing before they know if the day will be kind.

They greet the morning not with certainty, but with courage.
They offer their song as an act of faith.

This Gnomean Proverb reminds us that hope is not a response
to conditions, but a choice of spirit.
You can sing even when you do not know how the day will
unfold.

At the Church of Gnome, we believe joy can be a prelude, not
just a result.
To begin with song is to shape the day's story rather than wait
for it.

Let your voice rise before the outcome is clear.
That is the power of living with open wings.

Gnome Blessings.

The gnome who cements every answer builds a house with no windows.

At first the walls feel strong, sturdy, protective.
But soon the air grows stale, the light fades, and the view of the wider world disappears.

This Gnomean Proverb reminds us that certainty can become a prison.
To lock every question into fixed answers may feel safe, but it also seals you off from wonder.
Mystery cannot breathe in a house without windows.

At the Church of Gnome, we believe wisdom requires open spaces.
It means leaving room for questions, for fresh air, for light to filter in from beyond what you already know.
Answers can guide, but they must never harden into cages.
Every soul needs windows, wide enough to see the horizon.

Do not cement yourself in.
Build your house with openings for curiosity.
Let the winds of mystery move freely through it.

Gnome Blessings.

Communion with gnomes begins where certainty ends and curiosity kneels.

It is not achieved by force or proof.
It begins with wonder, humility, and openness.

This Gnomean Proverb reminds us that the sacred cannot be approached with arrogance.
It asks for respect, for listening, for the softening of your own agenda.

At the Church of Gnome, we believe real communion is always an invitation, not a demand.
To kneel before mystery is to enter into dialogue with it.

Step forward with humility.
Let curiosity guide you.
That is where communion begins.

Gnome Blessings.

Your shadow doesn't disappear when ignored, it just learns to whisper.

Silence does not dissolve it.
Neglect only makes it subtler and harder to trace.

This Gnomean Proverb reminds us that avoidance is not healing.
The parts of yourself you refuse to face still live within you, shaping your words and choices.

At the Church of Gnome, we believe wholeness begins with acknowledgment.
To listen to the whisper is to reclaim your own power.

Do not fear the shadow.
Turn toward it.
It is still part of you, waiting to be heard.

Gnome Blessings.

Skipping the pain is skipping the portal.

What you try to leap over becomes the threshold you never
cross.
Pain, when faced, is passage.

This Gnomean Proverb reminds us that suffering is not the
goal, but it is often the teacher.
It is the path through which transformation walks.

At the Church of Gnome, we believe courage is not avoiding the
wound, but moving through it with presence.
Only there do you find the other side of yourself.

Do not rush past the pain.
Enter it.
It may be the doorway you've been searching for.

Gnome Blessings.

You are not a speck in the cosmos. You are a breath it is holding.

You are not lost in vastness.
You are carried by it.
You are its living exhale.

This Gnomean Proverb reminds us that smallness does not mean insignificance.
You are both tiny and infinite, held and holding, a piece of the great whole.

At the Church of Gnome, we believe the universe is intimate.
It breathes through you even as you breathe it in.
You are not separate from the sacred vastness.

Feel the breath.
Know you are its rhythm.

Gnome Blessings.

Guilt has no place at joy's table.

It poisons the meal and dims the light.
Joy cannot flourish in the presence of self-punishment.

This Gnomean Proverb reminds us that happiness is not
something you must earn.
It is not a reward for perfection.
It is a birthright of being alive.

At the Church of Gnome, we believe joy is sacred and deserves a
clear place in your life.
Let go of guilt when you enter its presence.
Sit freely.
Receive its nourishment.

Gnome Blessings.

A rested spirit sings clearer songs.

Exhaustion muffles your voice and distorts your tune.
Rest gives it resonance again.

This Gnomean Proverb reminds us that creativity and clarity
come from restoration, not depletion.
Stillness and sleep are part of the sacred rhythm.

At the Church of Gnome, we believe rest is holy practice.
It renews your strength and returns you to your natural melody.

Stop.
Breathe.
Let your spirit find its voice again.

Gnome Blessings.

Anger held too long becomes a home you never meant to live in.

It settles into your walls.
It colors your days.
It becomes a shelter that traps rather than protects.

This Gnomean Proverb reminds us that anger is meant to pass
through, not to be your address.
When held too long, it reshapes you into its image.

At the Church of Gnome, we believe release is a form of self-
care.
Let the anger teach you, then let it leave.
Do not build your dwelling from its fire.

Open the door.
Step outside.
The world is larger than your anger.

Gnome Blessings.

Just because you've learned to live with the thorn doesn't mean you should keep it.

Adaptation is not the same as healing.
Survival is not the same as wholeness.

This Gnomean Proverb reminds us that pain can become so
familiar it feels normal.
But what is endured is not always what is meant to remain.
The thorn does not prove your strength.
It simply waits for you to release it.

At the Church of Gnome, we believe courage is not only bearing
the wound but choosing to seek its removal.
Freedom begins when you stop mistaking pain for destiny.

You are allowed to let go of what hurts, even if you've learned to
live with it.

Gnome Blessings.

Symbols speak what language cannot hold.

They carry weight beyond words.
They bridge the gap between seen and unseen.

This Gnomean Proverb reminds us that symbols are more than decoration.
They are vessels of meaning, carrying truths too vast for ordinary speech.

At the Church of Gnome, we believe sacred symbols matter because they bypass the limits of logic.
They speak directly to the soul, stirring memory, mystery, and belonging.

When words falter, trust the symbol.
It is language of its own.

Gnome Blessings.

Sit beside them in silence, that is the prayer.

Words are not always needed.
Presence itself can be blessing enough.

This Gnomean Proverb reminds us that companionship often speaks more deeply than explanation.
Silence shared with love carries more weight than speeches of comfort.

At the Church of Gnome, we believe prayer is not only spoken.
It is lived in the quiet, in the listening, in the being-with.

Do not worry about saying the right thing.
Your nearness is already holy.

Gnome Blessings.

Sorry is a spell when spoken without defense.

It softens the hardest ground.
It begins the work of repair.
It creates space where healing can take root.

This Gnomean Proverb reminds us that apology loses its power when wrapped in excuses.
But spoken with humility and no defense, it becomes transformative.

At the Church of Gnome, we believe true apology is sacred offering.
It acknowledges harm and invites restoration.
It is magic of the heart.

Speak it simply.
Let the spell work.

Gnome Blessings.

The river does not judge. It only carries.

It does not demand perfection of what it holds.
It accepts stone, leaf, and branch alike, moving them toward the sea.

This Gnomean Proverb reminds us that life flows without condemnation.
The river of existence is not interested in worthiness; it is interested in movement.

At the Church of Gnome, we believe grace is like the river.
It does not wait for you to be flawless before holding you.
It carries you as you are, onward, always onward.

Trust the river.
Let it hold you.
Its current does not ask who you are, only that you allow yourself to flow.

Gnome Blessings.

A still gnome sees more than a wandering king.

The king travels far, yet his gaze is restless.
The gnome remains rooted, and the whole world arrives to meet him.

This Gnomean Proverb reminds us that vision does not always come from motion.
Clarity comes when the heart grows quiet, when the eyes learn to notice what rushing overlooks.
Stillness reveals truths that distance and conquest cannot.

At the Church of Gnome, we believe stillness is its own form of power.
It is the throne of those who refuse to be distracted by endless striving.
The gnome, though small and unmoving, perceives more than the king who crosses mountains without ever seeing the moss beneath his feet.

To be still is not to be idle.
It is to allow wisdom to emerge.
It is to see the sacred where others rush past.

Be still, and let the world reveal itself.

Gnome Blessings.

Not every wound wants a cure, some just want company.

Pain does not always need fixing.
Sometimes it only needs to be witnessed, honored, and held.

This Gnomean Proverb reminds us that rushing to heal can
dishonor the depth of grief.
The wound may not be ready to close; it may only be ready to be
acknowledged.

At the Church of Gnome, we believe presence is a sacred gift.
You do not need to mend everything.
You need only to stay, to listen, to sit with the ache.

Healing often begins not with solutions, but with
companionship.

Gnome Blessings.

The deepest rest is remembering you were never meant to be at war with yourself.

Self-criticism exhausts more than labor.
Inner conflict drains more than any task.

This Gnomean Proverb reminds us that peace begins within.
When you end the battle against yourself, you reclaim the energy to live fully.

At the Church of Gnome, we believe self-compassion is sacred ground.
You were not created to be your own enemy.
You were created to walk gently with yourself, as you would with another.

Lay down the weapons.
Let rest return to you.
Peace with yourself is the truest restoration.

Gnome Blessings.

A soul at war sees only enemies; a soul at peace sees kin everywhere.

Conflict within projects conflict without.
The battles we refuse to resolve inside ourselves become the lens through which we see the world.

This Gnomean Proverb reminds us that perception begins within.
If we cultivate peace in our own soil, we will find it sprouting even in unexpected places.
If we neglect it, we will see hostility even in a friend's face.

At the Church of Gnome, we believe peace is not passive; it is active cultivation.
It begins inward, but its harvest is shared outward.
The one who tends peace within the self becomes a wellspring of kinship in the world.

Seek reconciliation inside.
The world will follow.

Gnome Blessings.

If your kindness comes with strings, it's a leash, not a gift.

What looks generous may still bind another in obligation.
What sounds caring may still control.

This Gnomean Proverb reminds us that real generosity is free of
hidden demands.
It liberates, not restrains.
It blesses without expecting return.

At the Church of Gnome, we believe sacred kindness never
disguises control.
Love frees.
Compassion releases.
Anything else is not gift, but tether.

Offer without strings.
Only then is kindness true.

Gnome Blessings.

What visits you at night may be memory in disguise.

Dreams often carry the weight of what has been.
They return not as history, but as symbols, shadows, whispers.

This Gnomean Proverb reminds us that the subconscious is a keeper of stories.
Even when forgotten by the mind, the soul remembers.
What rises in the night is often a fragment of your own becoming, asking to be heard.

At the Church of Gnome, we believe dreams can be sacred messengers.
Some are prophecy, some are memory, some are the soul's attempt to heal itself.

Listen closely.
The night may be speaking in memory's clothing.

Gnome Blessings.

To see a ghost is to glimpse how thin the veil truly is.

It is a reminder that presence does not end with the body, that the story continues beyond what we can measure.
The ghost lingers as echo, as memory, as love refusing to be silenced.

This Gnomean Proverb reminds us that the boundaries we draw between life and death are softer than we think.
To encounter a ghost is not merely to fear; it is to recognize how much of existence is unseen, and how close it remains.

At the Church of Gnome, we believe the veil is not wall but curtain.
Sometimes it lifts in grief, sometimes in longing, sometimes in mystery, but always to remind us that connection endures.

Do not fear the ghost.
It comes to teach that love outlasts absence.

Gnome Blessings.

Your story began long before your birth.

The blood you carry.
The traditions you inherit.
The wounds and wisdom of those who came before.

This Gnomean Proverb reminds us that life is not an isolated spark.
It is a continuation, a chapter in a book that began generations ago.

At the Church of Gnome, we believe ancestry is not just history; it is living presence.
You are shaped by their choices, their songs, their prayers, their struggles.
And now you add your own words to the unfolding story.

Honor those before you.
Carry the story forward with care.

Gnome Blessings.

Some revolutions begin with a seed, not a sword.

Change does not always roar.
Sometimes it grows quietly, rooted in patience, breaking the ground slowly.

This Gnomean Proverb reminds us that transformation need not be violent to be powerful.
The seed holds a strength sharper than any blade.
It creates not destruction, but renewal.

At the Church of Gnome, we believe the greatest revolutions are those that bring life, not death.
They are seeded in love, nurtured with time, and harvested in justice.

Plant the seed.
It may be the revolution the world most needs.

Gnome Blessings.

The gnome speaks to stones the way others pray.

To them, every stone is alive, listening, carrying memory.
What others overlook, the gnome reveres.

This Gnomean Proverb reminds us that sacredness is not
limited to the lofty.
It lives in what is solid, simple, and silent.
Even stone holds spirit, if you know how to listen.

At the Church of Gnome, we believe reverence belongs
everywhere.
To pray is not only to lift words to the sky.
It is also to bow low to the ground and speak to what endures.

Speak to the stones.
They have been listening longer than you have lived.

Gnome Blessings.

What comes through you is not yours, it's everyone's blessing.

The song, the kindness, the vision; they are not meant to be hoarded.
They arrive through you so they can flow outward.

This Gnomean Proverb reminds us that we are vessels, not vaults.
The sacred moves through us so the world can be nourished.
To cling to it as possession is to block its purpose.

At the Church of Gnome, we believe gifts are communal.
What blesses you is meant to bless others.
Your offering multiplies when it is shared.

Let it flow through.
It was never yours alone.

Gnome Blessings.

A gift given to be witnessed is not a gift but a mirror seeking applause.

It does not flow outward freely; it circles back to feed the ego.
True giving does not demand recognition.

This Gnomean Proverb reminds us that generosity becomes
hollow when tangled with vanity.
A gift is sacred only when it seeks nothing in return.

At the Church of Gnome, we believe giving is an act of humility.
It honors the other.
It honors the world.
It does not need the echo of praise to prove itself.

Give without the mirror.
Give so that love, not applause, is multiplied.

Gnome Blessings.

Shine weird, so the others can find you.

Your strangeness is a beacon.
Your oddness is a signal fire for the ones searching for kin.

This Gnomean Proverb reminds us that authenticity is not just for you.
It creates connection.
It lights the path for those who thought they were alone.

At the Church of Gnome, we believe uniqueness is holy.
To dim your weirdness is to hide the very thing that might save another's spirit.
Let it shine, and the ones who need it will gather.

Do not hide the light of your strangeness.
It may be the lantern someone else has been waiting to see.

Gnome Blessings.

Each day you choose the garden over the poison, the roots remember your courage.

Every decision to nurture instead of neglect writes itself into
the earth.
The soil carries memory.
The roots carry story.

This Gnomean Proverb reminds us that small daily choices
matter more than grand gestures.
The ground records them.
The future grows from them.

At the Church of Gnome, we believe courage is not always loud.
It is often the quiet decision to choose life, to choose care, to
choose love.

The roots remember.
And they will reward your faithfulness with growth.

Gnome Blessings.

Believe not because it's proven, but because it whispers true.

Certainty is not the soil of faith; resonance is.
Truth often arrives quietly, without evidence, yet carrying undeniable weight.

This Gnomean Proverb reminds us that proof is not the only measure of reality.
The heart knows things the mind cannot chart.
The whisper of truth is often more trustworthy than the shout of logic.

At the Church of Gnome, we believe faith lives in the space beyond proof.
It honors the intuition, the resonance, the quiet sense that something is real because it speaks deeply to the soul.

Listen for the whisper.
It may be the truest voice of all.

Gnome Blessings.

Quick answers fade, but hard-won wisdom roots itself forever.

What comes easily often slips away just as quickly.
But the truths discovered through struggle, through reflection,
through experience; these hold fast.

This Gnomean Proverb reminds us that depth cannot be rushed.
The tree that grows slowly becomes the strongest; the lesson
that costs us something becomes the one we never forget.

At the Church of Gnome, we believe wisdom ripens in its own
time.
Patience, humility, and endurance shape it more than brilliance
ever could.
It is the rooted knowledge, not the fleeting fact, that nourishes
generations.

Do not chase the quick answer.
Welcome the slow truth.
It will remain when all else fades.

Gnome Blessings.

To look up is not to escape, but to align.

The sky is not an exit from the world, it is a reminder of its
vastness.
The heavens do not pull you away from the earth; they draw
you deeper into its meaning.

This Gnomean Proverb reminds us that wonder is not
avoidance.
It is connection.
When you lift your gaze, you are not abandoning the ground.
You are remembering that it, too, belongs to the cosmos.

At the Church of Gnome, we believe reverence is not a turning
away but a tuning in.
The stars do not call you to leave, but to live more fully aligned
with what is infinite.

Look up, and know you are already part of what you see.

Gnome Blessings.

Some hands shaped you without ever holding you.

An ancestor's choice.
A stranger's word.
A sacrifice made in silence.

This Gnomean Proverb reminds us that influence travels
beyond touch.
Lives intersect in ways we may never know, molding us
through unseen acts.

At the Church of Gnome, we believe gratitude must stretch
backward and outward.
You are not only the product of your own effort.
You are the fruit of choices made long before and far away.

Honor the unseen hands.
They shaped you, even without holding you.

Gnome Blessings.

You are not unkind for protecting your peace.

Boundaries are not cruelty.
Rest is not selfishness.
Distance is not betrayal.

This Gnomean Proverb reminds us that peace is a treasure too
valuable to be surrendered to every demand.
You cannot pour from an empty vessel, nor heal from constant
depletion.

At the Church of Gnome, we believe peace is sacred
stewardship.
Protecting it allows you to live with clarity, to love with
wholeness, to give without collapse.

Hold your peace gently, but guard it firmly.
It is holy ground.

Gnome Blessings.

The unspoken always finds another way to speak.

Silence does not erase truth.
It only diverts it into shadows, gestures, and hidden fractures.

This Gnomean Proverb reminds us that truth is persistent.
If denied a voice, it will seep through body, tone, or
circumstance until it is acknowledged.

At the Church of Gnome, we believe honesty is mercy.
It prevents unspoken pain from festering.
It clears the air before silence hardens into distance.

Speak gently, but speak.
The truth will find its way, but better to give it words than let it
carve its message in harder places.

Gnome Blessings.

Some bonds are not made, they are remembered.

The recognition is instant, like a spark between two lives that have always known one another.
What feels like chance meeting is often memory surfacing.

This Gnomean Proverb reminds us that connection does not always begin in the present.
Some ties stretch back through time, across stories and lifetimes, waiting for the right moment to return.

At the Church of Gnome, we believe the soul remembers what the mind forgets.
Love, kinship, and belonging often carry the scent of eternity.
To meet again is to remember.

Trust the bonds that feel ancient.
They are.

Gnome Blessings.

Neglect rarely shouts, it erodes.

It works slowly, quietly, until what once felt strong begins to crumble.
What is ignored fades long before it breaks.

This Gnomean Proverb reminds us that absence of care is itself a kind of harm.
It is the steady wearing down of what was meant to endure.

At the Church of Gnome, we believe attention is sacred labor.
Relationships, work, the spirit, the earth; all thrive only when tended.
Without care, even the strongest will weaken.

Do not wait for collapse.
Give your presence now.

Gnome Blessings.

They see through the masks and love the soul beneath.

Pets do not care for titles, appearances, or the costumes we wear for the world.
They sense the truth of us; the tiredness, the joy, the ache, the essence.

This Gnomean Proverb reminds us that animals meet us in our rawest form.
They do not require performance.
They do not withhold affection for imperfection.
They love what is real, not what is staged.

At the Church of Gnome, we believe pets are sacred companions because they teach unconditional seeing.
Their gaze bypasses every mask, resting only on the soul that beats beneath.
They remind us that being loved as we are is not only possible, it is already happening.

Trust the eyes that see you truly.
They belong to the ones who have always loved without condition.

Gnome Blessings.

Even the tallest tree bows to time.

What stands mighty now will one day return to soil.
What rises high will one day lie low.
Nothing resists the rhythm forever.

This Gnomean Proverb reminds us that impermanence is not
tragedy.
It is balance.
It is the cycle that keeps life renewing itself.

At the Church of Gnome, we believe humility is the wisdom
time teaches all.
Strength is not found in resisting change, but in bowing to it
gracefully.
Even the mighty must bend, and in bending, they find peace.

Do not fear the bowing.
It is part of being alive.
Time is not your enemy.
It is your teacher.

Gnome Blessings.

The gnome trusts the pull before he sees the trail.

The way forward is not always visible.
The map unfolds only when the first step is taken.

This Gnomean Proverb reminds us that guidance often comes
as tug before clarity.
The heart knows before the path reveals itself.

At the Church of Gnome, we believe trust is the lantern in
uncertainty.
To follow the pull is to honor the unseen wisdom leading you.
The trail appears for those willing to walk before they
understand.

Trust the pull.
The path will come.

Gnome Blessings.

Plan not just for success, but for sustainability.

A moment of triumph is fleeting.
A lasting foundation is what carries generations.

This Gnomean Proverb reminds us that success without
endurance quickly crumbles.
It is not enough to reach the summit if the ground beneath is
weak.
True wisdom looks beyond the moment, building what can
withstand time.

At the Church of Gnome, we believe sacred work is measured
not in how fast it rises, but in how well it endures.
The garden is not judged by the first bloom, but by the soil that
continues to give.

Do not only plan to succeed.
Plan so that what you grow will nourish long after you are gone.

Gnome Blessings.

No pedestal is more sacred than the patch of earth we all stand on.

Exaltation may lift one, but it cannot hold the weight of all.
The ground, steady and shared, is the true holy place.

This Gnomean Proverb reminds us that equality is written into the soil.
We rise and fall together, always bound by the earth beneath us.
The sacred is not above, but beneath our feet.

At the Church of Gnome, we believe reverence begins with humility.
To kneel to the earth is to honor the source of all life.
To treat the ground as holy is to remember that no one stands higher than another.

Do not seek the pedestal.
Seek the soil.
That is where sacredness lives.

Gnome Blessings.

Time is the only coin you cannot earn back, so spend it where your soul belongs.

Every moment given is gone forever, whether wasted or cherished.
The choice is not whether you will spend, but how.

This Gnomean Proverb reminds us that time is the truest form of wealth.
Unlike money, it cannot be stored.
Unlike possessions, it cannot be reclaimed.
What you give your time to reveals your devotion, your values, your very soul.

At the Church of Gnome, we believe presence is sacred currency.
To spend time on what nourishes, uplifts, and aligns with the deepest truths of your being is to invest in eternity.
To squander it on hollow pursuits is to impoverish the spirit.

Guard your coin.
Spend it wisely.
Your soul already knows where it belongs.

Gnome Blessings.

The final lantern is never blown out, it is handed on.

Life does not end in darkness.
The flame you carried is passed into other hands, other hearts,
other lives.

This Gnomean Proverb reminds us that death is not erasure.
It is transition.
The light moves forward, illuminating paths for those who
remain.

At the Church of Gnome, we believe every life is a lantern.
The glow may change form, but it is never lost.
It continues, carried by memory, by legacy, by spirit.

Your lantern will not vanish.
It will shine in others.
It will guide beyond your own time.

Gnome Blessings.

Nature is not your backdrop it is your kin.

The forest is not scenery.
The river is not stage decoration.
They are relatives, alive with their own breath and story.

This Gnomean Proverb reminds us that we do not stand above
the natural world.
We belong to it.
We are one thread in its living web.

At the Church of Gnome, we believe reverence for the earth is
reverence for family.
To harm it is to wound your kin.
To honor it is to honor yourself.

Look again at the trees, the sky, the soil.
They are not background.
They are brothers, sisters, companions.

Gnome Blessings.

Desire bends the truth more quickly than reason can straighten it.

The heart longs, and in longing it reshapes reality to fit its hunger.
What is wanted often masquerades as what is true.

This Gnomean Proverb reminds us that passion is powerful, but it can also distort.
Reason may correct in time, but desire moves faster, curving perception before logic can arrive.
This is not cause for shame, but for vigilance.

At the Church of Gnome, we believe truth must be held gently, with awareness of how easily we twist it.
Desire is not enemy; it is compass, but it must be tempered by humility and honesty.
To see clearly, you must question not only what you fear, but what you most want.

Be wary of desire's illusions.
Seek the truth beneath the longing.

Gnome Blessings.

The storm tests not the sky but the readiness of the traveler.

Thunder does not ask permission.
Winds do not wait for comfort.
The storm is not trial of the heavens; it is measure of your preparation.

This Gnomean Proverb reminds us that challenge is not personal punishment.
Life's tempests arrive on their own schedule.
What matters is not whether storms come, but whether you are ready to face them with steadiness and wisdom.

At the Church of Gnome, we believe resilience is not avoidance of storms, but readiness for them.
To walk in awareness, to carry tools of patience and courage, is to transform the storm from terror into teacher.

The sky will do what it will.
Your readiness is the only thing you carry.

Gnome Blessings.

Waiting for their apology keeps you in their story.

The absence of their words becomes the chain that binds you.
Their silence becomes the script you are forced to keep
repeating.

This Gnomean Proverb reminds us that healing is not
dependent on another's courage.
It is born from your own choice to step free.
Their apology may never come, but your freedom can still
begin.

At the Church of Gnome, we believe forgiveness is not always
reconciliation; it is release.
It loosens their hold on your life, even if their silence continues.
It allows you to write new chapters in your own story.

Stop waiting at the door of their remorse.
Walk into your own life.

Gnome Blessings.

Still waters soothe the feet, yet no gnome mistook a pond for the ocean.

Rest has its place, but it is not the fullness of the journey.
Calm refreshes, but vastness transforms.

This Gnomean Proverb reminds us that moments of peace are
gifts, but they are not the whole horizon.
The pond comforts, but it cannot carry you.
The ocean asks for courage, and in return, it grants depth.

At the Church of Gnome, we believe balance is sacred.
Rest when the waters are still.
But do not confuse comfort for completion.
The ocean still waits.

Soak your feet, then rise.
There is more yet to be discovered.

Gnome Blessings.

True power lies not in being seen, but in seeing.

Visibility may draw attention, but perception transforms lives.
The eyes that notice, that understand, that honor; these carry
the deeper strength.

This Gnomean Proverb reminds us that recognition from others
fades quickly.
But the ability to recognize the sacred in them lasts forever.

At the Church of Gnome, we believe vision is holier than
spectacle.
To see another clearly is to give them dignity.
To see the world truthfully is to live awake.

Do not crave being seen.
Learn instead to see.
That is power.

Gnome Blessings.

The melt always remembers what winter tried to hide.

Snow covers, conceals, softens the harsh edges.
But when thaw comes, what was buried is revealed again;
sometimes tender, sometimes broken, but always true.

This Gnomean Proverb reminds us that concealment is only
temporary.
Time uncovers all, whether secrets, wounds, or truths.
The thaw does not judge; it simply reveals.

At the Church of Gnome, we believe honesty is inevitable.
What we bury may sleep through seasons, but it cannot be kept
forever.
The melt returns, and with it the opportunity to face what was
hidden with new eyes.

Do not fear the thaw.
It does not come to condemn, but to uncover what is ready to be
seen.

Gnome Blessings.

Only brittle branches refuse to bend when the wind brings new wisdom.

The living tree sways.
The flexible limb survives.
The rigid one breaks.

This Gnomean Proverb reminds us that wisdom requires
adaptability.
New truths will come, and only those willing to bend will grow
from them.
Resistance to learning is the path to fracture.

At the Church of Gnome, we believe humility is strength.
To bend is not to be weak.
It is to be alive.
It is to allow the winds of insight to shape you into something
stronger.

Let the winds come.
Bend, and you will stand.

Gnome Blessings.

Peace spoken calmly walks further than fury shouted loud.

Anger burns hot, but quickly.
It scorches the moment, while peace continues its journey long after the echo of fury has faded.

This Gnomean Proverb reminds us that true strength does not need volume.
The calm voice may seem soft, but it carries farther, planting itself where rage only ricochets.

At the Church of Gnome, we believe peace is not passivity but power.
Its force is steady, patient, enduring.
It does not demand attention; it creates transformation.

Choose the calm word.
It will outlast the loud one.
It will walk further than you ever imagined.

Gnome Blessings.

To guard the vulnerable is to keep the lantern lit for all.

The flame of safety burns brightest where the fragile are protected.
When we shield those who cannot shield themselves, the whole circle shines.

This Gnomean Proverb reminds us that strength is not measured by what we can take, but by what we protect.
Justice is not privilege; it is responsibility.
When the vulnerable are neglected, the light dims for everyone.

At the Church of Gnome, we believe compassion is a communal fire.
When it burns for one, it warms all.
When it is extinguished for the least, the night grows darker for the rest.

Guard well.
Keep the flame steady.
Your care lights the path for more than you will ever see.

Gnome Blessings.

It is better to share bread in honesty than feast in stolen halls.

The simplest meal in peace nourishes more than the richest banquet born of deceit.
Food tastes hollow when served on a foundation of harm.

This Gnomean Proverb reminds us that dignity sweetens every bite.
The spirit cannot be fooled into joy when the table is laid with arrogance or greed.
Simplicity with integrity is always more filling than abundance tainted by pride.

At the Church of Gnome, we believe sustenance is more than bread; it is trust, it is fairness, it is peace.
To eat honestly is to be fed fully.
To eat dishonestly is to remain hungry, no matter how heavy the feast.

Choose the smaller table, if it is honest.
That is where true nourishment lives.

Gnome Blessings.

The path shapes the walker, and the company shapes the path.

No road is walked alone.
Even your solitary steps are imprinted by those who came
before and those who walk beside.

This Gnomean Proverb reminds us that we are both shaped and
shaping.
The stones beneath your feet wear your story, even as they
reshape your stride.
And the companions beside you, wise or foolish, kind or cruel,
bend the path itself with their presence.

At the Church of Gnome, we believe journey and community are
inseparable.
You do not walk untouched by your path, nor do you walk
without leaving your mark upon it.
Together, the path and its company write your becoming.

Step carefully.
Choose your companions well.
Both will shape who you are.

Gnome Blessings.

You are allowed to be both the shelter and the thunder.

Gentleness and power are not enemies.
They live side by side within you.

This Gnomean Proverb reminds us that authenticity means wholeness.
You do not need to choose only one face.
You are allowed to protect, and you are allowed to shake the ground.

At the Church of Gnome, we believe the soul carries multitudes.
To embrace them is not contradiction, but truth.
There is wisdom in your calm, and there is wisdom in your storm.

Be the shelter when love calls for gentleness.
Be the thunder when justice calls for strength.
Both are holy.

Gnome Blessings.

You owe nothing to what harmed you.

Not your silence.
Not your loyalty.
Not your return.

This Gnomean Proverb reminds us that freedom begins with
release.
To break from harm is not betrayal; it is survival.
You do not need to keep feeding the hand that wounded you.

At the Church of Gnome, we believe dignity means walking
away from what diminishes your soul.
No chain of obligation binds you to your pain.
You are free to step beyond it.

You owe nothing.
You are already enough.
Your life belongs to you.

Gnome Blessings.

You cannot plant joy in soil watered with denial.

Happiness cannot grow where truth is starved.
Pretending does not nourish.
Avoidance does not bloom.

This Gnomean Proverb reminds us that joy requires honesty.
Only when the soil is watered with truth can anything lasting
take root.

At the Church of Gnome, we believe denial is poison to the
garden of the spirit.
To face what is real, even when it hurts, is to prepare the
ground for joy.

Do not cover over what aches.
Name it.
Water the soil with truth.
Then joy will grow.

Gnome Blessings.

To lend your voice to the voiceless is to double their strength.

Silence is heavy, but it grows lighter when voices rise beside it.
Your words do not replace theirs; they create room for their
own to be heard more clearly.

This Gnomean Proverb reminds us that power grows when it is
shared.
When your voice joins the call for dignity, it does not
overshadow; it harmonizes.
Together, voices weave a fabric too strong to be torn apart.

At the Church of Gnome, we believe solidarity is sacred.
The lantern burns brighter not because one flame consumes
another, but because many flames shine together.
Each voice keeps the circle stronger, each echo widening the
space where truth can stand.

Do not stay silent when silence is crushing.
Add your voice; not to speak over, but to strengthen the chorus
already rising.

Gnome Blessings.

You don't have to understand the stars to feel their light.

Knowledge is not the only doorway into wonder.
The mystery shines whether you can explain it or not.

This Gnomean Proverb reminds us that awe does not require comprehension.
The sacred does not demand your mastery; it asks only your presence.

At the Church of Gnome, we believe reverence begins when you allow yourself to be touched by what is greater than you.
To feel the light is enough.
To be moved by it is holy.

Let the stars shine.
Let their mystery be gift, not problem.
Feel their light, and let that be your understanding.

Gnome Blessings.

Failure plants seeds success rarely touches.

It humbles, reshapes, and softens the soil.
It teaches patience and endurance in ways triumph never can.

This Gnomean Proverb reminds us that failure is not barren ground.
It is fertile with lessons, with resilience, with hidden wisdom.

At the Church of Gnome, we believe failure is a sacred teacher.
It opens paths that victory alone cannot.
It grows humility, courage, and a deeper kind of strength.

Do not despise failure.
It is planting something in you that success cannot.

Gnome Blessings.

A torn cloak does not diminish the soul it covers; worth is not measured in coin.

Outer appearances deceive.
What looks ragged may conceal radiance.
What looks poor may hold treasures unseen.

This Gnomean Proverb reminds us that dignity is not defined
by wealth or clothing.
The soul is untouched by fabric, untouched by gold.
Its value is inherent, eternal, unbought.

At the Church of Gnome, we believe every being carries worth
beyond measure.
To judge by coin or cloth is to blind yourself to the truth of
spirit.

See past the cloak.
See the soul.
Its light has never been diminished.

Gnome Blessings.

A word can heal like water or wound like stone; choose what your mouth will carry.

The tongue is a vessel.
It pours what the heart holds: gentleness or cruelty, blessing or curse.

This Gnomean Proverb reminds us that language is never neutral.
Every word spoken enters the world as gift or as wound.
The speaker always decides which it will be.

At the Church of Gnome, we believe words are sacred instruments.
Like water, they can cleanse, refresh, and revive.
Like stone, they can strike, bruise, and break.
The difference lies only in the intention of the tongue.

Guard your vessel.
Let your words flow like water.
Leave the stones behind.

Gnome Blessings.

The breath you take was once a leaf's.

The inhale you claim as your own was first released by the green world.
Life is a circle of exchange, a covenant written in air.

This Gnomean Proverb reminds us that existence is shared.
You do not breathe alone.
Every breath is gift, passed from tree to lung, from leaf to body, from creation into creation.

At the Church of Gnome, we believe gratitude begins with breath.
To inhale is to receive blessing.
To exhale is to give it back.
The sacred is woven into every cycle of air.

Breathe with reverence.
Every breath is proof that you belong to the whole.

Gnome Blessings.

Close encounters begin within; the universe responds to the frequency of your intent.

Contact is not first an outer event, but an inner alignment.
The cosmos listens to the tone of your heart more than the sound of your words.

This Gnomean Proverb reminds us that reaching outward without preparing inward is like calling across the stars with a closed spirit.
Intention shapes the signal.
Clarity sharpens the connection.
Peace makes the invitation safe.

At the Church of Gnome, we believe communion with the greater mysteries is not about control but resonance.
When you tune yourself to openness, curiosity, and love, the universe recognizes you.
It responds not to demand, but to sincerity.

Set your inner frequency.
Let your intent carry light.
And know that the encounter begins the moment you align within.

Gnome Blessings.

It is easy to look back with shame.

To see only the missteps.
To dwell on the times you wish had gone differently.

But this Gnomean Proverb reminds us that the past version of
you was not your enemy.
They were your companion.
They carried the weight you could not yet name.
They kept walking even when the road was unclear.

At the Church of Gnome, we believe gratitude must extend both
outward and inward.
You are not here in spite of your past self.
You are here because of them.
Even their mistakes were part of the path that shaped your
becoming.

You do not need to honor every choice.
But you can honor the courage it took to keep going.
You can thank the one who got you to this threshold.

The person you were held the lantern.
Now you hold it.
And you will hand it on to the next you, brighter still.

Gnome Blessings.

A secret in the wrong hands is a seed thrown to the wind.

What could have taken root in trust scatters into places it was
never meant to grow.
Soon the story is no longer yours, and its fruits no longer kind.

This Gnomean Proverb reminds us that trust is sacred soil.
A secret entrusted to those who honor it becomes safe, held,
and fertile.
But given carelessly, it becomes gossip, rumor, and distortion.
What was once intimate becomes a weapon.

At the Church of Gnome, we believe discretion is not silence
born of fear but reverence born of love.
To hold what is entrusted to you is to guard the integrity of
another's spirit.
To betray it is to abandon not only them, but yourself.

Plant wisely.
Choose soil that will hold, not scatter.

Gnome Blessings.

To see only opinion and not the person is to mistake the cloak for the soul.

A viewpoint may be loud, may be troubling, may even feel like a wall between you.
But beneath the opinion is a being made of the same breath, the same mystery, the same fragile hope as you.

This Gnomean Proverb reminds us that no one is defined entirely by what they think or what they argue.
Opinions are garments; sometimes chosen with care, sometimes inherited, sometimes worn out or ill-fitting.
The soul beneath remains deeper, older, and far more sacred than any cloak it wears.

At the Church of Gnome, we believe compassion means looking past the outer layers.
It means remembering that before belief, there was birth.
Before opinion, there was essence.
To reduce someone to their cloak is to miss the vastness of who they are.

See the person before you, not only the view they carry.
Disagree with the cloak if you must, but do not mistake it for the whole.
The soul is always more.

Gnome Blessings.

Kindness is lighter than fear, yet strong enough to carry it.

Fear weighs down, gripping the chest and clouding the mind. But even the smallest act of kindness; offered or received, can lift that burden, even if only for a moment.

This Gnomean Proverb reminds us that gentleness is not weakness.
It is strength of a subtler kind, able to bear what terror alone cannot overcome.
Fear shrinks, but kindness expands.
It creates space wide enough for courage to breathe.

At the Church of Gnome, we believe kindness is the most durable of powers.
It does not break under pressure.
It carries weight without complaint.
It shifts the atmosphere around it like light breaking through clouds.

When fear presses heavy, answer with kindness.
It will not erase the burden, but it will give you the strength to carry it.

Gnome Blessings.

False blame stains the accuser more deeply than the accused.

The one targeted may be wounded, but the wound of dishonesty embeds itself in the soul of the accuser.
Their words echo back, carrying shame long after the moment passes.

This Gnomean Proverb reminds us that lies reveal more about the speaker than the one they condemn.
Accusation without cause is confession in disguise; a confession of fear, of envy, of hidden wounds.

At the Church of Gnome, we believe justice is not only about defending the innocent but also about refusing to corrupt ourselves in the name of harm.
Every false word spoken drags the soul further from its own light.

Do not be quick to accuse.
Truth will speak for itself.
Let your tongue stay clean of shadows.

Gnome Blessings.

A voice asking for help is not broken; it is a bell calling the village to remember its strength.

Need is not weakness; it is reminder.
It summons connection, compassion, and shared responsibility.

This Gnomean Proverb reminds us that asking is not failing.
It is courage, and it invites others into their humanity.

At the Church of Gnome, we believe help is sacred exchange.
The one who calls out and the one who answers are both strengthened.
The bell rings, and all are invited to respond.

Do not silence your need.
Let it ring.
The village is waiting.

Gnome Blessings.

Tread lightly, laugh often, and guard the gardens of your soul.

Life is tender ground, and joy is its best fertilizer.
Without laughter, the soil grows dry.
Without protection, weeds take root.

This Gnomean Proverb reminds us that the soul needs both playfulness and care.
It thrives in balance; gentle steps, frequent joy, and mindful boundaries.

At the Church of Gnome, we believe tending the soul is daily practice.
Not in severity, but in delight.
Not only in discipline, but in laughter.

Guard your garden.
Fill it with lightness.
It will bloom all the more for it.

Gnome Blessings.

The rain does not ask who deserves to be cleansed.

It falls on all alike; the weary and the proud, the broken and the whole.
It does not pause to measure worthiness, nor stop to question who has earned refreshment.

This Gnomean Proverb reminds us that mercy is not rationed by desert.
The sacred gives freely, without calculation, because that is its nature.
The gift of rain is grace itself; abundant, impartial, unreserved.

At the Church of Gnome, we believe the sky is teacher.
It teaches us to pour without prejudice, to nourish without judgment, to give without strings.
Every drop is reminder that love is not diminished by being shared widely; it is fulfilled.

Let yourself be cleansed.
Let others be cleansed beside you.
The rain does not ask questions; it simply blesses.

Gnome Blessings.

Wisdom enters first through listening, then takes root in living.

The ear is the doorway, but the steps must still be taken.
Words heard but not lived remain surface knowledge, like seeds
scattered on stone.

This Gnomean Proverb reminds us that wisdom requires both
openness and practice.
The humble ear receives.
The willing life enacts.
Only when both join together does wisdom grow strong and
enduring.

At the Church of Gnome, we believe wisdom is not measured by
how much you know, but by how much you embody.
Listening is sacred posture.
Living is sacred action.
Together they make truth flesh.

Listen deeply.
Live honestly.
That is how wisdom takes root.

Gnome Blessings.

Your spirit has an audience beyond the veil.

The ancestors listen in the quiet.
The unseen companions lean close when you whisper, when you grieve, when you rejoice.
Your life is not unnoticed; you are witnessed, even when you feel alone.

This Gnomean Proverb reminds us that presence is greater than what our eyes can confirm.
The boundary between here and beyond is thin, and your spirit is never speaking into silence.
What you live reverberates across unseen realms.

At the Church of Gnome, we believe you are part of a community that stretches across time.
Those who came before you, those who walk beside you, those who will come after you; each is linked by threads the veil cannot cut.
To live with awareness of this is to remember you are always in company, always in conversation with eternity.

Speak your truth.
Lift your song.
The audience is already gathered.

Gnome Blessings.

We all kneel to plant seeds and rise to greet the sun. No one stands taller than another in the garden of life.

Every being is humbled by the soil.
Every being is lifted by the same light.

This Gnomean Proverb reminds us that equality is not theory; it
is woven into the act of living.
To kneel and to rise are shared rituals.
The garden accepts no hierarchy.

At the Church of Gnome, we believe dignity belongs to all.
No one's hands are too clean for the soil, and no one's head too
high for the sun.
We share the same ground.
We share the same light.

The garden remembers only how we grew together.

Gnome Blessings.

Go within, not to escape the world, but to greet it more truthfully.

The inner path is not retreat, it is preparation.
Silence does not sever your ties with life; it strengthens them.

This Gnomean Proverb reminds us that the soul is not a cave for hiding, but a forge for refining.
To journey inward is not to abandon the outer world, but to return to it with clearer eyes, steadier steps, and a heart more aligned with truth.

At the Church of Gnome, we believe the inner and outer are reflections of one another.
The stillness you cultivate inside becomes the clarity you carry outside.
The deeper you go within, the more authentically you can meet the world without masks, without noise, without fear.

Do not run away; go in.
Find what is real.
Then come back ready to live it.

Gnome Blessings.

You are not too much, you are finally not pretending.

The weight was never in your being; it was in the shrinking you
forced upon yourself.
Your fullness was always waiting to be seen.

This Gnomean Proverb reminds us that authenticity may feel
overwhelming at first, but only because the world has grown
used to your silence.
The truth of you is not excess.
It is exactly what was needed.

At the Church of Gnome, we believe the soul was never meant to
live in fragments.
To embody your wholeness is not arrogance; it is liberation.

Do not dim.
Do not shrink.
Be fully yourself.
It was always enough.

Gnome Blessings.

Some people are not bridges, they are mirrors.

They may not carry you forward, but they reflect you back to yourself.
Their role is not passage, but revelation.

This Gnomean Proverb reminds us that relationships serve different purposes.
Some take you across thresholds.
Others simply show you who you are.

At the Church of Gnome, we believe both are sacred.
The bridge carries you onward.
The mirror anchors you in truth.
Neither is wasted.

Honor the mirrors.
They teach you what you most need to see.

Gnome Blessings.

Peace is the flame. Boundaries are the lantern.

Without the lantern, the flame burns out too quickly.
Without the flame, the lantern holds only emptiness.

This Gnomean Proverb reminds us that peace and boundaries
must walk together.
Peace without boundaries is fragile.
Boundaries without peace are hollow.
Together they protect and sustain what is sacred within you.

At the Church of Gnome, we believe boundaries are not walls,
but vessels.
They guard the light so it can keep shining.
They ensure that peace is not stolen by every passing wind.

Keep your flame alive.
Build the lantern around it.
Both are needed for the light to endure.

Gnome Blessings.

You weren't ready because love never plans for parting.

Love always imagines more time, more words, more days.
Separation feels unnatural because love was never meant to end.

This Gnomean Proverb reminds us that grief is not failure to prepare.
It is proof that love was real.
Readiness for loss is an illusion, because love does not train for absence.

At the Church of Gnome, we believe mourning is sacred testimony.
It says, "I loved, and I still love."
The pain is not weakness, but the echo of devotion.

Do not fault yourself for not being ready.
No one is.
Love never rehearses goodbye.

Gnome Blessings.

To betray trust is to poison your own well.

The harm may seem aimed outward, but it circles back, seeping into the ground you yourself must drink from.
The betrayal of another is also the betrayal of your own integrity.

This Gnomean Proverb reminds us that trust is not simply exchanged; it is shared.
When we break it, the fracture spreads in all directions, staining not only the relationship but the very spirit of the betrayer.

At the Church of Gnome, we believe every act of trust is sacred.
It is water drawn from a shared well.
To protect it is to keep both hearts alive.
To taint it is to thirst even as the bucket is full.

Guard the well.
Keep the water clear.
For you will drink from it, too.

Gnome Blessings.

The gnome stumbles often, and still reaches the garden.

The path is uneven, full of roots, shadows, and turns.
Falling is part of the journey, not proof of failure.

This Gnomean Proverb reminds us that progress is not
measured by how gracefully you walk, but by your willingness
to keep moving.
Even the missteps carry you closer.
Even the stumbles teach you how to rise again.

At the Church of Gnome, we believe the destination is never
denied to those who persist.
The garden is patient.
It welcomes the weary, the clumsy, the delayed.
The important thing is not to walk perfectly, but to keep
walking.

Stumble if you must.
The garden will still be waiting.

Gnome Blessings.

Let new things carry old wisdom.

Innovation without roots forgets its purpose.
Tradition without renewal forgets its breath.
Together they sustain one another.

This Gnomean Proverb reminds us that wisdom is not meant to
stay frozen in the past.
It is meant to flow into the present, to guide what is new, to
shape what is yet to come.

At the Church of Gnome, we believe balance is found in
honoring what was while welcoming what will be.
The old offers depth.
The new offers vitality.
When they walk together, both remain alive.

Do not cling only to what has been.
Do not rush only toward what is new.
Let them meet, and let life flourish.

Gnome Blessings.

Ears closed to advice soon walk paths that collapse beneath them.

The ground may look solid, but without the wisdom of others, the traveler misses the cracks.
What pride ignores, humility could have prevented.

This Gnomean Proverb reminds us that no one sees the road in its entirety.
Another's vision, another's story, another's warning may save you from a stumble you cannot see yourself.

At the Church of Gnome, we believe counsel is not weakness; it is strength.
To listen is to borrow the sight of many.
To refuse is to walk blind on a fragile path.

Open your ears.
Let wisdom widen your way.

Gnome Blessings.

The higher arrogance climbs, the lower it stumbles.

Pride builds towers but forgets to build foundations.
It rises quickly, but the fall is inevitable, and the ground waits
without pity.

This Gnomean Proverb reminds us that true strength is not in
elevation but in grounding.
The higher the spirit climbs without humility, the greater the
distance of its collapse.

At the Church of Gnome, we believe humility is the steadying
root beneath all growth.
Without it, greatness topples under its own weight.
With it, even the highest branches sway safely in the wind.

Do not climb without roots.
Pride may rise, but it cannot stand.

Gnome Blessings.

Regret is heavy, but beginning is always lighter.

To carry what you did not do, what you left undone, what you postponed, becomes a weight on the soul.
But the moment you begin, the burden shifts.
Action lifts what inaction only deepens.

This Gnomean Proverb reminds us that the cure for regret is not perfection but motion.
The first step is already a release.
The smallest beginning outweighs the heaviest delay.

At the Church of Gnome, we believe life is merciful.
It does not require flawless starts.
It asks only for willingness to move, to try, to take the first step again and again.

Begin now.
The weight will lift.

Gnome Blessings.

What you feel without proof is often more real than what you see.

Sight can deceive.
Appearance can mask.
But the body and soul know truths the eyes cannot hold.

This Gnomean Proverb reminds us that intuition and resonance
are sacred forms of knowing.
The unseen often carries more truth than the visible.
The whisper is often clearer than the shout.

At the Church of Gnome, we believe proof is not the only path to
wisdom.
The heart has its own evidence.
The spirit has its own way of recognizing what is real.

Trust what you feel.
It may be the clearest truth you will ever know.

Gnome Blessings.

We are quick to trap people in old versions of themselves.

The mistake they made.
The season they stumbled.
The shadow they once carried.

But this Gnomean Proverb reminds us that identity is not a prison.
It is a river, always moving, always reshaping the stones it touches.
No one is fixed forever in the person they were yesterday.

At the Church of Gnome, we believe that change is not only possible, it is sacred.
Forgiveness is not naïve; it is trust in the truth that growth is real.
Compassion is not blindness; it is vision that sees beyond what was into what could be.

To honor who someone may become does not erase accountability.
It simply refuses to let their past be the only story told.
It holds the door open for transformation, even when doubt lingers in the frame.

You are not the worst thing you have done.
You are not the limits of your failures.
You are the living possibility of renewal, of shedding, of beginning again.

The past shaped you, but it does not own you.
The future waits for your next becoming.

Gnome Blessings.

Carrying another's anger is like tending a fire whose smoke chokes your own lungs.

What begins as their flame soon becomes your suffocation.
You breathe in what was never yours to hold.

This Gnomean Proverb reminds us that we are not called to
carry the weight of another's fury.
Compassion does not mean inhaling poison.
Love does not require letting yourself be consumed by smoke.

At the Church of Gnome, we believe boundaries are sacred acts
of care.
You may sit with another in their fire, but you must not let it
steal your breath.
You can witness without carrying.
You can love without burning.

Step back from the smoke.
Let them tend their own flame.

Gnome Blessings.

Roots do not argue with rivers; they simply drink and grow.

The tree does not debate the flow; it receives what comes, takes what is given, and lets growth follow naturally.

This Gnomean Proverb reminds us that wisdom is often found not in resistance, but in receptivity.
Life offers streams of nourishment: advice, experience, truth.
To argue with them is to wither; to accept them is to thrive.

At the Church of Gnome, we believe harmony with the sources of life is itself an act of strength.
The roots teach us to bow, to receive, and to grow without contention.

Drink deeply.
Grow quietly.
The river is enough.

Gnome Blessings.

The leprechaun hides gold so you remember laughter is the true treasure.

The chase, the trick, the shimmering promise of riches; it is all misdirection, all a riddle meant to expose our hunger.
What remains after the search is not the gold, but the grin.

This Gnomean Proverb reminds us that the sacred gift is not in what glitters, but in what gladdens.
We are meant to laugh at the chase, to find joy in the trick, to realize the treasure was never the prize but the spirit that pursued it.

At the Church of Gnome, we believe delight is its own form of wealth.
Gold may vanish, but laughter echoes.
Coins rust, but joy renews itself endlessly.
The leprechaun hides the gold to reveal the greater truth: it was never what you needed.

Remember to laugh.
That is the treasure that cannot be stolen.

Gnome Blessings.

Your soul already knows, your mind just catches up.

Wisdom is not something you discover; it is something you remember.
The spirit moves ahead, while thought lingers behind, piecing together what the heart has already seen.

This Gnomean Proverb reminds us that intuition is not guesswork.
It is the deeper knowing that precedes explanation.
The mind will find its way, but the soul is already there.

At the Church of Gnome, we believe trust in the soul is trust in the eternal.
Its voice is ancient, carrying memory older than thought.
Follow it, and let the mind catch up in time.

The soul leads.
The mind learns.
Both are needed, but one is always first.

Gnome Blessings.

The smallest refusal can shift a mountain.

It may be just one word, no, spoken softly, perhaps trembling,
but firm.
Yet that word carries the weight of generations, breaking a
chain that seemed unbreakable.

This Gnomean Proverb reminds us that transformation is not
always grand or loud.
Sometimes it begins in a single choice: to stop, to resist, to step
aside from the path that harm demands.
The mountain of old patterns, of inherited wounds, of heavy
silence, trembles when even one person dares to refuse.

At the Church of Gnome, we believe courage is often quiet.
You do not need to shout to move the world.
You only need to choose truth over fear, even in the smallest of
acts.

Your refusal is not weakness.
It is an earthquake in disguise.
Do not underestimate the mountain-shifting power of a single
no.

Gnome Blessings.

A cracked pot lets the moonlight in.

Perfection holds little beauty.
It is the fracture that makes space for radiance to shine
through.

This Gnomean Proverb reminds us that brokenness is not the
end of usefulness.
It may be the very place where light enters.
Your cracks are not shame; they are openings.

At the Church of Gnome, we believe wholeness includes
imperfection.
The vessels that shine brightest are the ones marked by time,
by use, by struggle.
The crack is not the flaw.
It is the window.

Let your fractures glow.
They are proof that light can find its way in.

Gnome Blessings.

Even the unmoved stone becomes covered in moss.

Stillness is not the same as stagnation.
Life continues, even when nothing seems to change.

This Gnomean Proverb reminds us that time softens
everything.
The hardest stone is eventually cloaked in green.
The slowest season still carries its quiet transformations.

At the Church of Gnome, we believe growth does not always
look dramatic.
Sometimes it is subtle, almost hidden, but no less real.
Even what feels unchanging is still part of the cycle of
becoming.

Do not despair if your progress feels slow.
Trust the moss.
It is proof that life has never stopped moving through you.

Gnome Blessings.

Laughter echoes longer in temples than chants do.

It rolls off stone walls, lingers in memory, and softens even the heaviest hearts.
The sacred is not diminished by joy; it is amplified by it.

This Gnomean Proverb reminds us that reverence is not always solemn.
The divine is just as present in laughter as in ritual.
The spirit delights in play as much as it dwells in prayer.

At the Church of Gnome, we believe joy is holy ground.
A smile can be worship.
A laugh can be blessing.
Together they create a sound that sanctifies the air.

Do not fear to laugh in sacred spaces.
It is the echo the temple was built to carry.

Gnome Blessings.

To be small is not to be lesser, it is to be closer to the roots.

The seed is tiny, yet it carries forests within.
The root is hidden, yet it holds the tree in place.

This Gnomean Proverb reminds us that greatness is not always tall or loud.
It is often near the soil, close to the source, resting in what sustains.

At the Church of Gnome, we believe the lowly places are holy.
Smallness is not weakness; it is intimacy with the ground of being.
The nearer you are to the roots, the closer you are to the strength that feeds all life.

Do not despise smallness.
It may hold the greatest power of all.

Gnome Blessings.

If you lie to your reflection, don't be surprised when it lies back.

Deception turns inward before it turns outward.
What you refuse to face will always distort what you see.

This Gnomean Proverb reminds us that honesty with yourself is the ground of all clarity.
When you choose illusion, your own image becomes stranger to you.
When you choose truth, even your flaws can become teachers.

At the Church of Gnome, we believe authenticity is the beginning of wisdom.
No mask will hold forever.
The reflection always remembers what the mind tries to forget.

Speak the truth to yourself.
Even if it trembles, even if it hurts.
That honesty will be the mirror that sets you free.

Gnome Blessings.

Even righteous anger needs release before it rots.

Anger may rise from justice, from love, from the refusal to tolerate harm.
But when it lingers too long, it ferments into bitterness, choking the heart that carried it.

This Gnomean Proverb reminds us that anger has a purpose but not a permanent place.
It can ignite change, move us to act, clarify what matters most.
Yet once its work is done, it must be set down.
Otherwise, the flame that once guided will consume.

At the Church of Gnome, we believe anger is a teacher, not a companion for life.
Honor its lesson, thank it for its spark, then let it go before it poisons the well of your spirit.

Hold it too long, and it will rot within you.
Release it, and you will find the ground made fertile for peace.

Gnome Blessings.

To deprogram is to begin again with kindness.

Unlearning is not punishment.
It is liberation.
It is making space for gentleness to replace the voices of fear.

This Gnomean Proverb reminds us that the hardest patterns are
not broken by shame, but by compassion.
You cannot berate yourself into freedom.
You must soften into it.

At the Church of Gnome, we believe transformation comes
when cruelty, whether from within or from others, is replaced
with patience.
To begin again with kindness is to return to the truth of your
being.

Let the old programming fade.
Rewrite yourself with tenderness.

Gnome Blessings.

Your ego hates to be laughed at. That's why it needs it.

Pride swells in seriousness.
It shrinks when faced with joy.

This Gnomean Proverb reminds us that humor is not just relief;
it is medicine.
A laugh at your own expense keeps you from worshiping the
mask of self-importance.

At the Church of Gnome, we believe the soul grows lighter when
the ego is humbled.
Laughter restores balance, reminding you that you were never
meant to live as an idol to yourself.

Laugh at the ego.
It will sting, but it will also heal.

Gnome Blessings.

If you can't sit still, ask what you're running from.

Restlessness is often escape in disguise.
The body fidgets, but it is the soul that is unsettled.

This Gnomean Proverb reminds us that silence reveals what
noise tries to cover.
Stillness unmasks the fears we keep fleeing.

At the Church of Gnome, we believe movement is not always
progress.
Sometimes the truest growth happens in stillness, when you
finally face what chases you.

Sit.
Listen.
What you fear may be smaller than you imagined.

Gnome Blessings.

The tree spirit teaches patience, for it measures time in centuries, not seasons.

Its wisdom is not hurried.
It does not rush to bloom or panic when leaves fall.
It waits, rooted, certain that time is an ally, not an enemy.

This Gnomean Proverb reminds us that growth is slow, and that slowness is sacred.
The tree spirit does not demand immediate fruit; it trusts the cycles, the rains, the winters, the centuries.
Patience is not passive; it is partnership with the rhythm of the earth.

At the Church of Gnome, we believe to walk with trees is to remember what endurance looks like.
Their patience humbles our frantic striving, reminding us that what matters most takes lifetimes to unfold.
The tree spirit is not idle; it is listening, growing, and remembering in a language longer than ours.

Learn from the tree spirit.
Stand steady.
Let your roots measure time by centuries, not seasons.

Gnome Blessings.

If your gnome disappears, it's not lost, it's on a quest.

Absence does not always mean abandonment.
Sometimes it is simply a chapter unfolding beyond your sight.

This Gnomean Proverb reminds us that mystery often
accompanies devotion.
What looks like loss may be purpose.
What feels like departure may be journey.

At the Church of Gnome, we believe the unseen path is still
sacred.
The gnome that wanders is still faithful.
Its steps carry meaning even when you cannot follow.

Trust the quest.
The story is not over.

Gnome Blessings.

When moss is your cushion, even the hardest stone becomes a throne.

Comfort does not come from wealth or grandeur; it comes from perspective.
The smallest softness can transform the heaviest burden.

This Gnomean Proverb reminds us that humility and gratitude turn difficulty into blessing.
The throne is not defined by gold, but by the spirit that sits upon it.

At the Church of Gnome, we believe the sacred often dresses itself in simplicity.
A patch of moss may hold more grace than any palace chair.

Sit gently.
See differently.
Even stone can feel like royalty when gratitude is your cushion.

Gnome Blessings.

Do not dim to make others shine, stand beside them.

Your light is not competition.
It is companionship.
When lights stand together, the night becomes brighter for all.

This Gnomean Proverb reminds us that shrinking yourself
serves no one.
The world does not grow richer when you go unseen.
It grows richer when every lantern burns fully, side by side.

At the Church of Gnome, we believe community thrives in
shared brilliance.
No one is diminished by another's glow.
True belonging is when each light is allowed to shine freely,
together.

Do not hide.
Do not shrink.
Stand tall, and let the light of others join yours.

Gnome Blessings.

To search for cryptids is to admit the world is not yet finished.

These elusive beings dwell in the margins of our maps, in the gaps of certainty, in the wilds where imagination still has room to breathe.

This Gnomean Proverb reminds us that mystery is not failure of knowledge, but proof that life still carries secrets.
To chase the hidden creature is to confess that wonder remains, that the earth has more chapters than we have read.

At the Church of Gnome, we believe the pursuit of the unknown is itself sacred.
Whether cryptids walk the forest or live only in story, they remind us that the world is larger, stranger, and richer than our measurements.

Do not demand every shadow be explained.
Let some mysteries remain wild.
They keep the story alive.

Gnome Blessings.

The mind is a lantern; whatever it shines on grows brighter.

Where attention rests, energy flows.
What you choose to illuminate expands, whether it be fear or
hope, bitterness or gratitude.

This Gnomean Proverb reminds us that reality is not only
discovered; it is shaped.
The light of your mind magnifies whatever it lingers upon, and
soon the path reflects your focus.

At the Church of Gnome, we believe thought is a sacred tool, a
flame that can either guide or consume.
You cannot stop the lantern from shining, but you can choose
where to direct its beam.
This choice is the quiet work of creation itself.

Shine wisely.
The world around you is shaped by what your lantern reveals.

Gnome Blessings.

The body bends beneath the weight the mind refuses to set down.

Stress, fear, grief; what we do not release in thought sinks into flesh.
The shoulders slump, the stomach churns, the breath shortens under invisible burdens.

This Gnomean Proverb reminds us that the mind and body are not separate realms, but one field.
The heaviness you carry in thought becomes tension in bone and muscle, shaping you even as you try to ignore it.

At the Church of Gnome, we believe sovereignty of body and mind is one principle, not two.
To tend your thoughts is to honor your body.
To soothe your body is to quiet your mind.
Peace must touch both or it is incomplete.

Set down what you no longer need.
Your body has been carrying it all along.

Gnome Blessings.

What you see depends on where you're standing and whether your eyes are open.

Perspective shapes perception.
Blindness is not always in the eyes, but in the willingness to see.

This Gnomean Proverb reminds us that reality is never fixed.
It shifts with angle, with openness, with humility.
The same scene can appear as obstacle or opportunity depending on where you stand.

At the Church of Gnome, we believe wisdom requires movement.
To see fully is to shift your stance, to open your heart, to let your eyes be widened by new light.

Stand elsewhere.
Open wider.
You may see more than you thought was there.

Gnome Blessings.

Whether you whisper to trees or speak on stages, you're still a person with mud on your boots and stars in your eyes.

Fame or obscurity does not change the truth of your being.
You remain both earthly and cosmic, humble and infinite.

This Gnomean Proverb reminds us that identity is not defined by setting.
You are the same soul whether hidden in the forest or standing in the spotlight.

At the Church of Gnome, we believe grounding and wonder belong together.
Mud keeps you rooted.
Stars keep you reaching.
Both live within you at all times.

Do not forget the mud.
Do not forget the stars.
You were always both.

Gnome Blessings.

The inner eye sees farther than the outer.

The body's eyes measure distance and form, but the spirit's eye perceives meaning.
It reaches beyond walls and horizons, touching truths that sight alone cannot hold.

This Gnomean Proverb reminds us that perception is more than vision.
The unseen is as real as the seen, and the soul has its own way of knowing.
To trust the inner eye is to trust the whisper that speaks before evidence, the vision that arises before proof.

At the Church of Gnome, we believe clarity comes not only from observation but from attunement.
Remote sight, intuition, the sudden knowing; these are not accidents.
They are glimpses through the lens of the inner eye, a window into the larger pattern.

Close your outer eyes when they distract you.
Let the inner one open.
It will show you more than distance ever could.

Gnome Blessings.

What you tend in others blooms beyond you.

Every word of encouragement, every act of care, every seed of kindness takes root in soil you may never see.
The garden grows wider than the gardener's eyes.

This Gnomean Proverb reminds us that your influence is not limited to your own life.
What you nurture in another continues long after the moment has passed.
It carries into their choices, their relationships, their future.

At the Church of Gnome, we believe generosity multiplies.
The bloom you inspire may shade and feed generations beyond your reach.
The smallest tending may ripple into fields of abundance.

Tend carefully.
The harvest will travel further than you imagine.

Gnome Blessings.

Yesterday and tomorrow drink from the same well.

What you call past and future are not distant strangers, but siblings drawing water from the same source.
The well does not dry when names change; it flows beneath them all.

This Gnomean Proverb reminds us that time is not a straight path, but a circle of return.
Moments echo into one another.
The memory of yesterday informs the hope of tomorrow, and both live within the same present.

At the Church of Gnome, we believe the well is eternity itself, disguised as days and years.
To drink deeply now is to taste both what has been and what will come.
The water has always been the same, even as our hands have changed.

Do not divide your life into rigid compartments of before and after.
Drink from the well.
It is one, and it is here.

Gnome Blessings.

Every scar you tend teaches someone else they're not alone.

Healing is never just for you.
The moment you choose care, you light the path for others carrying wounds of their own.

This Gnomean Proverb reminds us that scars carry stories.
To tend them with tenderness is to make those stories safe to share.
Your survival becomes proof of possibility.

At the Church of Gnome, we believe healing is communal.
When you treat your own pain with compassion, you are also softening the world around you.
Your example whispers, "This too can be endured, and mended."

Tend your scars.
They are not only reminders of what hurt, but testaments of what healed.

Gnome Blessings.

The trees never ask you to explain yourself.

They do not demand justification before they offer shade.
They do not need proof before they grant you breath.

This Gnomean Proverb reminds us that belonging in the
natural world is unconditional.
You are accepted simply because you are alive.

At the Church of Gnome, we believe the earth teaches us what
community should be.
No endless proving.
No endless earning.
Only welcome, only presence.

Let the trees remind you:
you are enough without explanation.

Gnome Blessings.

Sit with their sorrow until it no longer feels alone.

Do not rush to fix, or to mend, or to silence.
Let presence itself be the balm.

This Gnomean Proverb reminds us that sorrow softens when it is shared.
The weight may not vanish, but it becomes bearable when another chooses to stay.

At the Church of Gnome, we believe companionship in pain is sacred.
It honors the wound, even when it cannot yet heal.
It says: you are not abandoned in this.

Stay long enough.
Let your presence carry what words cannot.

Gnome Blessings.

A story told with missing chapters cannot guide the traveler to truth.

Without the full telling, the wisdom is distorted.
The listener is left wandering with half a map.

This Gnomean Proverb reminds us that honesty in storytelling
is essential.
To omit the difficult, the flawed, the broken is to rob the story
of its power.

At the Church of Gnome, we believe truth requires wholeness.
The shadows must be named along with the light.
Only then can the story serve as true guide.

Tell the whole story.
Even the parts that ache.
Especially the parts that ache.

Gnome Blessings.

The elders knew things the internet forgot.

Their wisdom was carved in memory, carried in story, passed
hand to hand across generations.
They did not need a search bar to remember what mattered.

This Gnomean Proverb reminds us that not all knowledge is
data.
Information is abundant, but wisdom is rare.
The elders carried rhythms of living, lessons born of time,
truths that do not trend.

At the Church of Gnome, we believe reverence for the past is not
nostalgia; it is balance.
The internet may store information, but the elders store
experience.
The two together can guide us, but only if we honor the
memory keepers still among us.

Listen to them.
Their voices carry maps no screen will ever show.

Gnome Blessings.

Sasquatch is less a beast to find than a mirror showing how little we know of wildness.

We search the forests with traps and cameras, convinced that discovery means capture.
Yet the greater mystery is not whether Sasquatch walks among the trees, but what its story reveals about our own estrangement from the untamed.

This Gnomean Proverb reminds us that myth and mystery are not distractions from truth; they are keepers of it.
The image of Sasquatch unsettles us because it confronts how far we have drifted from wildness, from silence, from reverence for the unknown.
In chasing the creature, we are really chasing our lost intimacy with the living world.

At the Church of Gnome, we believe the question of Sasquatch is less about evidence and more about humility.
It is the reminder that there are beings, realms, and rhythms beyond our control.
It teaches that the world is larger than our definitions, that wonder cannot be domesticated, and that wilderness itself is holy.

Perhaps the real encounter is not with footprints in the mud but with the awareness that we are still guests in a world we barely understand.
Perhaps the true sighting is not of a shadow between trees but of our own reflection; small, fragile, and needing to remember how to bow before the forest again.

Sasquatch is not only a question about wildness; it is a mirror.
And the mirror is asking if we are willing to become wild enough to see.

Gnome Blessings.

The river does not rehearse its song.

It flows as it is, unpracticed, unpolished, and still beautiful.
Its music is born of movement, not preparation.

This Gnomean Proverb reminds us that life does not require
perfection before it is shared.
The song of your soul is not meant to be rehearsed endlessly.
It is meant to flow, raw and alive.

At the Church of Gnome, we believe authenticity is greater than
performance.
Like the river, your truth carries power simply by moving
forward.
You do not need to wait until it sounds perfect.
You only need to let it be heard.

Flow as you are.
Your song is already enough.

Gnome Blessings.

When you hear the stream singing, it is the Undines reminding you to flow instead of resist.

Their voices shimmer in ripples, urging you to move with the current instead of damming it.
To resist is to stagnate.
To flow is to live.

This Gnomean Proverb reminds us that water knows the secret of endurance: it yields, yet it carves stone; it bends, yet it always arrives.
The Undines embody this truth, teaching us that movement with grace is stronger than rigidity with pride.

At the Church of Gnome, we believe water is a sacred teacher.
The spirit of the stream is not weakness; it is resilience.
To listen to the Undines is to remember that surrender is not defeat, but transformation.

When you hear the waters, bow to their wisdom.
They are singing the way forward.

Gnome Blessings.

The gnome who shouts at one fallen branch yet ignores the burning forest confuses noise for justice.

It is easy to make a scene over what is small while neglecting what is urgent.
Anger without perspective becomes distraction.

This Gnomean Proverb reminds us that justice is not about volume.
It is about clarity, proportion, and the courage to face the larger fire.
Noise can feel righteous, but it is hollow if it avoids what truly matters.

At the Church of Gnome, we believe discernment is sacred.
Energy is limited, and justice demands it be placed where the need is greatest.
To chase every fallen twig while the forest burns is to abandon wisdom.

Do not mistake shouting for service.
Lift your voice where the fire calls for it most.

Gnome Blessings.

Your energy is sacred, give it with intention, not obligation.

Every act you offer carries your essence.
To give without care drains both you and the one receiving.
To give with presence becomes nourishment for both.

This Gnomean Proverb reminds us that generosity loses its
holiness when it is forced.
Obligation empties the heart.
Intention fills it with meaning.

At the Church of Gnome, we believe energy is life itself.
It is not infinite, and it is not meant to be squandered.
To offer it wisely is to honor yourself and those you serve.

Give when your spirit aligns with the act.
Hold back when it does not.
This is how your giving remains sacred.

Gnome Blessings.

Step lightly through a fairy circle, for it is both threshold and trick.

What seems like a ring of mushrooms is a gate, and every gate asks something of you.
It may offer wonder, or it may ask caution, but never indifference.

This Gnomean Proverb reminds us that the sacred often disguises itself in play.
The fairies tempt us not to harm, but to test whether we will pause long enough to honor what lies beneath the ordinary.
To walk carelessly is to miss the invitation.
To step reverently is to enter the threshold.

At the Church of Gnome, we believe the world is stitched with hidden doorways.
Fairy circles, strange coincidences, moments of impossible beauty; each is both trick and teaching.
They ask whether we see mystery or only mushrooms, whether we bow or whether we mock.

Step lightly.
The circle is not just on the ground.
It is also within you.

Gnome Blessings.

A song shared by the fire warms the soul more than the flame.

The fire gives heat to the body, but the song gives life to the heart.
Its melody lingers long after the embers fade, carrying the memory of voices joined together.

This Gnomean Proverb reminds us that community nourishes deeper than comfort.
Warmth without companionship is fleeting, but shared song ignites a different kind of flame; one that continues to glow inside us long after the night has grown cold.

At the Church of Gnome, we believe sacredness is found in the simple gatherings where joy is shared, where voices rise together, and where hearts remember their belonging.

Tend your fire, but tend also your song.
The flame fades, but the warmth of the soul endures.

Gnome Blessings.

You can't punish your past self into healing.

Shame does not mend wounds.
It only carves them deeper.

This Gnomean Proverb reminds us that the younger version of
you was doing the best they could with what they knew.
To heal them is not to condemn, but to understand.

At the Church of Gnome, we believe compassion is the key that
unlocks your own becoming.
Healing begins when you hold your past self gently, offering
the love they never received.
Punishment chains you to the pain.
Kindness frees you from it.

Lay down the whip of shame.
Pick up the balm of mercy.
That is how healing begins.

Gnome Blessings.

A single crumb of cake can sway the tide of a faerie's grudge.

What seems small to you may be weighty to another.
A token of kindness, even if ordinary, can transform
resentment into goodwill.

This Gnomean Proverb reminds us that gestures matter not by
size, but by spirit.
The faeries in our stories know this truth well: respect and
offering keep harmony alive.
The smallest gift, given sincerely, can mend what arrogance
would have shattered.

At the Church of Gnome, we believe the unseen responds to
reverence.
The same is true of the seen.
Kindness offered freely, even in crumbs, shifts the balance
toward peace.

Never dismiss the small gift.
It may be the very key that turns grudge into grace.

Gnome Blessings.

Restraint is the wisdom of those who see further.

The impulse demands action now, but vision looks beyond the moment.
It sees the ripple effect, the consequences, the lives touched by what may seem small today.

This Gnomean Proverb reminds us that strength is not always found in movement; it is often found in the pause.
To wait is not to lose.
It is to give time the chance to reveal what rushing would destroy.

At the Church of Gnome, we believe restraint is not about denial but about choosing clarity over urgency.
It is the space where wisdom has room to breathe.
It is the patience that allows your flame to last instead of burn out.

Hold yourself steady.
Do not confuse silence with weakness, nor patience with surrender.
Restraint is the lantern of those who see further down the path.

Gnome Blessings.

You do not need to climb the tree to hear its wisdom, just sit beneath it.

Its branches whisper to all who pause, not just to those who reach the highest boughs.
Its shade is teaching enough, if you will rest long enough to listen.

This Gnomean Proverb reminds us that wisdom is not always hidden in heights.
It is present at the roots, in the stillness, in the quiet invitation to stay near.

At the Church of Gnome, we believe the sacred is not earned by effort alone.
It is revealed through presence.
You do not have to ascend far to know what the tree already offers.

Sit in its shade.
Let the leaves speak.
The wisdom will come to you where you are.

Gnome Blessings.

The sacred enters when we show up with reverence.

It does not wait for ritual perfection or flawless words.
It waits for sincerity, for presence, for the quiet bow of the heart.

This Gnomean Proverb reminds us that the sacred is not barred by doors, nor limited to temples.
It flows where reverence is given, whether in forests, kitchens, or at the edge of your own breath.

At the Church of Gnome, we believe reverence is the true altar.
Without it, ritual is empty.
With it, even silence becomes holy.

Show up with humility.
Show up with awe.
The sacred will meet you there.

Gnome Blessings.

What you water every day will know your name.

Every act of care, however small, is recorded in the soil of life.
The garden bends toward the hand that tends it.
The soul softens in response to the practices that shape it over time.

This Gnomean Proverb reminds us that devotion is not built in grand gestures.
It is formed in the quiet rhythm of daily attention.
The things you nurture grow to recognize you, just as flowers lean toward the sun that warms them.

At the Church of Gnome, we believe the sacred honors constancy.
The rituals you repeat, the kindness you extend, the love you water; these are the seeds that become legacy.
Even when unnoticed, each drop carries meaning.

Tend wisely.
For what you water today will one day rise to meet you, whispering your name in gratitude.

Gnome Blessings.

The soul settles when the body is honored.

The spirit cannot find rest in a vessel that is despised or ignored.
To care for the body is to acknowledge it as sacred ground, the living temple where life itself breathes.

This Gnomean Proverb reminds us that peace is not reached only in the mind or heart.
It flows when body and spirit move together in harmony.
Rest, nourishment, movement, and tenderness are not distractions from holiness; they are the doorway to it.

At the Church of Gnome, we believe honoring the body is honoring the soul within it.
The sacred does not ask you to escape your flesh, but to cherish it.
It is the soil from which your spirit grows, the lantern that carries your flame.

Listen when the body asks for rest.
Feed it when it hungers.
Treat it with dignity, and your soul will find its stillness.

Gnome Blessings.

To ration affection as penalty is to poison the well you also must drink from.

Love withheld becomes corrosion, not correction.
What begins as punishment toward another eventually seeps
back into your own spirit.

This Gnomean Proverb reminds us that love is not a tool for
leverage.
It is not meant to be measured out as reward or withheld as
retribution.
To weaponize it is to wound the very bond it was meant to
sustain.

At the Church of Gnome, we believe affection must flow freely if
it is to remain pure.
To use it as punishment distorts its essence.
It teaches fear instead of trust, silence instead of intimacy.

Drink deeply of love without conditions.
Offer it even when you feel tempted to ration.
The well will stay clean only when the water is shared without
poison.

Gnome Blessings.

What you overlook is often what will save you.

It is the humble root beneath the soil, the unnoticed kindness,
the quiet whisper ignored in the rush of noise.
Life hides its lifelines in places we rarely think to look.

This Gnomean Proverb reminds us that salvation does not
always arrive with fanfare.
Sometimes it comes in stillness, in subtleties, in the presence
you have taken for granted all along.

At the Church of Gnome, we believe the sacred is woven into the
overlooked.
It is in the moss that cushions your steps, the stream that runs
unseen, the friend whose steady love carries you quietly
through the storm.

Look again at what you have dismissed.
It may already be carrying you.
It may already be your saving grace.

Gnome Blessings.

The inner world is not a hiding place. It is the forge.

It is where fire meets metal, where silence reshapes the soul, where reflection turns weakness into strength.

This Gnomean Proverb reminds us that retreat into the inner world is not escape, but preparation.
You do not withdraw to vanish; you withdraw to be refined.

At the Church of Gnome, we believe the work done within is holy labor.
The outer life draws its power from what was forged in the quiet chambers of the heart.
Without the inner fire, action becomes hollow.

Go inward, not to disappear, but to return transformed.
The forge will make you ready.

Gnome Blessings.

Start now. The soil forgives what you didn't plant.

It does not hold grudges for missed seasons.
It waits patiently for the seed you finally choose to give.

This Gnomean Proverb reminds us that regret for lost time is
unnecessary.
The earth does not dwell on what was withheld; it rejoices in
what is finally offered.

At the Church of Gnome, we believe it is never too late to begin.
Every act of planting carries its own season, its own harvest, its
own blessing.
The past may be gone, but the ground still longs for your care.

Do not wait for the perfect time.
Plant now.
The soil has already forgiven you.

Gnome Blessings.

The ones who left are not gone, they simply walk softer.

Their presence may no longer make noise, but it lingers in memory, in legacy, in the quiet places where love endures.

This Gnomean Proverb reminds us that absence is not emptiness.
Those who depart change form, but they do not vanish.
They walk in gentler rhythms, woven into the fabric of your days.

At the Church of Gnome, we believe love survives separation.
Death does not silence it, distance does not erase it, time does not dissolve it.
The ones who left simply move into subtler ways of being near.

Listen carefully.
In the silence you will hear their steps.
They are still with you, only softer now.

Gnome Blessings.

Fall forward, and bring back what you find.

The stumble is not wasted if it carries wisdom in its hands.
What feels like collapse is often discovery, a hidden doorway
only visible from the ground.

This Gnomean Proverb reminds us that failure is not an ending
but a form of gathering.
The forward fall places you closer to truths you could not see
from standing tall.
It humbles you, yes, but it also gives you treasures buried in the
soil.

At the Church of Gnome, we believe mistakes can be harvests.
The lessons gathered from falling often become nourishment
for the journey ahead.
Each bruise carries a map.
Each scar becomes a lantern.

Do not fear the fall.
Lean into it.
Collect what the ground has been holding for you, and rise
again carrying more than you had before.

Gnome Blessings.

Knowledge carried in the soul is treasure no hand can take.

Gold can be stolen, possessions can be lost, but the wisdom you embody cannot be taken from you.
It is the wealth that endures.

This Gnomean Proverb reminds us that true learning is not about accumulation of facts, but about transformation of self.
Once knowledge has shaped your spirit, it belongs to you forever.

At the Church of Gnome, we believe wisdom is the only inheritance that cannot be plundered.
It is the flame that lights every lantern, the treasure that enriches every journey, the wealth that outlives every possession.

Protect your wisdom.
Carry it humbly.
It is your truest fortune.

Gnome Blessings.

A stumble of the tongue leaves footprints longer than a stumble of the feet.

The body may recover from a fall, but careless words can echo far beyond the moment.
They travel into memory, shaping the path long after you've walked away.

This Gnomean Proverb reminds us that words carry power greater than we often realize.
A single slip can wound more deeply than years can heal.
Speech, once loosed, cannot be recalled.

At the Church of Gnome, we believe the tongue is sacred instrument.
To guard it is to walk wisely.
To let it wander without care is to leave footprints you may one day regret.

Speak slowly.
Speak gently.
Your words walk further than your feet.

Gnome Blessings.

To apologize well is to sweep the temple floor.

It clears the dust so that reverence can return.
It prepares the ground for sacredness to enter again.

This Gnomean Proverb reminds us that apology is more than words; it is work.
It is bending low, acknowledging what has been dirtied, and choosing to clean with humility.
A careless apology leaves debris behind.
A true apology makes the space ready for restoration.

At the Church of Gnome, we believe apology is not transaction but devotion.
It is the act of honoring the one you harmed by restoring what was broken.
It is the way we reopen the door to trust.

Sweep carefully.
Speak with sincerity.
Make the temple ready again.

Gnome Blessings.

The gnome bows not in certainty, but in wonder.

He does not kneel because he has solved the riddle of existence.
He bows because the mystery itself is holy.
The unanswered question is not a threat to him; it is an altar.

This Gnomean Proverb reminds us that reverence does not require mastery.
The sacred is not reserved for those who claim to know; it is open to those willing to marvel.
Certainty builds walls, but wonder opens doors.
The bow is not submission to fear; it is recognition of awe.

At the Church of Gnome, we believe humility is the heart of wisdom.
The gnome teaches us that the proper posture before mystery is not control, but reverence.
It is the willingness to admit that the world is larger than us, and that this largeness is a gift, not a punishment.
In bowing, the gnome affirms that what cannot be defined may still be cherished.

You do not need answers to be reverent.
You do not need certainty to bow.
Wonder alone is reason enough.

Gnome Blessings.

Wear your weird like it's blessed.

The quirks, the edges, the colors that do not blend; these are
not flaws, but signatures.
They mark you as one-of-a-kind, a presence the world has
never seen before.

This Gnomean Proverb reminds us that authenticity is a kind of
holiness.
What makes you unusual is what makes you luminous.
To hide your strangeness is to bury the lantern that others may
be looking for.

At the Church of Gnome, we believe uniqueness is sacred
offering.
The Divine delights in variety, in eccentricity, in the beauty of
difference.
Your weirdness is not a curse; it is the blessing only you can
bring.

Do not tuck it away.
Wear it proudly.
Let it be seen, and you will call others home to themselves.

Gnome Blessings.

Better flawed and true than polished and hollow.

The shine of perfection may dazzle for a moment, but it holds no warmth.
The cracked vessel may be rough, but it carries water honestly.

This Gnomean Proverb reminds us that truth, even with imperfections, is worth more than empty performance.
A false image may win applause, but it cannot nourish the soul.
Authenticity, even in its rawness, sustains.

At the Church of Gnome, we believe honesty is the holiest form of beauty.
It may not gleam, but it lasts.
It may not impress, but it heals.

Choose truth over polish.
Choose substance over shine.
Choose to be whole, even if you are imperfect.

Gnome Blessings.

When the lantern goes out, the path is remembered by the feet.

Light may fail, but memory of the way carries you onward.
The body recalls what the mind forgets, guiding you step by step.

This Gnomean Proverb reminds us that wisdom is not only external.
It is written in your being, carried in your movements, etched into the very rhythm of your life.
Even when vision fails, you are not lost.

At the Church of Gnome, we believe resilience means trusting the memory of the soul.
The path you have walked has shaped you, and that shaping remains.
Even in darkness, you are not without guidance.

Walk forward.
The path is already within your feet.

Gnome Blessings.

"Gnome Blessings" is the bow of one soul to another, honoring the mystery they both carry.

It is not a simple hello, farewell or casual phrase.
It is recognition: that you are sacred, that I am sacred, and that both of us walk within a mystery too vast to be contained.

This Gnomean Proverb reminds us that blessing is not about certainty; it is about reverence.
To say "Gnome Blessings" is to acknowledge that each person you meet carries hidden depths, unseen burdens, and unspoken wonders.
It is a bow to the soul, not the surface.

At the Church of Gnome, we believe words shape worlds.
To greet or send someone away with "Gnome Blessings" is to mark their path with light, to honor their journey without needing to define it.

Say it not lightly, but sincerely.
It is a bow of reverence, a recognition of the mystery that walks in us all.

Gnome Blessings.

The greatest victory is not over kingdoms, but over the unrest within.

Battles may win you land, titles, or fleeting recognition, but if your own spirit remains in turmoil, no conquest will satisfy. Peace within is the true crown, and only those who master themselves ever wear it.

This Gnomean Proverb reminds us that power without self-knowledge collapses.
The wars we fight outwardly are often mirrors of the conflicts we refuse to face inwardly.
Until you face your own unrest, no triumph can feel whole.

At the Church of Gnome, we believe sovereignty begins in the soul.
To calm the storm inside is to find a strength no sword can give and no enemy can take away.

Turn inward.
Win that war.
It is the only victory that endures.

Gnome Blessings.

Pain arrives uninvited, but suffering lingers only if we offer it a chair.

The ache of loss, the wound of disappointment, the sting of failure; these are part of being human.
But when we let them stay too long, giving them a place of honor in the house of our soul, pain transforms into suffering.

This Gnomean Proverb reminds us that grief and hurt are sacred visitors, but not permanent residents.
They come to teach, to humble, to soften; but not to rule.

At the Church of Gnome, we believe healing begins when we learn to let pain visit without letting it govern.
To acknowledge it is to honor truth.
To release it is to honor life.

Feel what you must, but do not build a throne for suffering.
Bow to its lesson, then let it go.

Gnome Blessings.

An untended mind becomes its own thief, stealing peace before the world ever can.

Left unattended, thoughts multiply into shadows, replaying
fears and rehearsing disasters that have not yet arrived.
The body is safe, but the mind convinces it otherwise.

This Gnomean Proverb reminds us that vigilance is not only
against outer dangers but against the chaos within.
The untrained mind robs sleep, joy, and presence long before
any enemy has touched us.

At the Church of Gnome, we believe tending the mind is sacred
labor.
Meditation, reflection, gratitude; these are the tools that guard
the treasury of peace.
To neglect them is to let the thief walk in unchallenged.

Keep watch.
Tend the garden of thought.
Do not let your own mind rob you of your rest.

Gnome Blessings.

To listen to the wind is to hear the world pray.

It carries the voices of trees bending, grasses swaying, rivers sighing.
Every current of air is a hymn, moving unseen yet felt in every breath.

This Gnomean Proverb reminds us that prayer is not limited to human tongues.
The world itself is always in prayer; offering, yearning, praising, grieving.
The wind is its messenger, weaving the petitions of earth into a song that never ends.

At the Church of Gnome, we believe listening is as holy as speaking.
When you stop to hear the wind, you hear the world remembering its connection to the unseen.
You are reminded that prayer is larger than words, older than temples, wider than creed.

Close your eyes.
Let the wind speak.
You will hear the whole earth praying through it.

Gnome Blessings.

The heart that counts its blessings never starves for happiness.

What you focus on multiplies, and gratitude turns even scarcity into abundance.
A thankful heart finds joy not by addition, but by recognition.

This Gnomean Proverb reminds us that happiness is not in the endless pursuit of more, but in the careful noticing of what already surrounds us.
The feast may be simple, but gratitude makes it rich.
The moment may be ordinary, but gratitude makes it radiant.

At the Church of Gnome, we believe gratitude is a sacred practice.
It transforms lack into sufficiency and sufficiency into joy.
A heart trained to count blessings will never starve.

Look around you.
Count again.
The table is fuller than you think.

Gnome Blessings.

The body is the soil, the mind its branches, and the soul the fruit; neglect one, and all wither.

These three are not separate; they are one living tree.
To dishonor the body is to weaken the mind.
To starve the mind is to sour the fruit of the soul.

This Gnomean Proverb reminds us that wholeness requires balance.
Health, clarity, and spirit must be tended together, each feeding the other, each sustained by care.

At the Church of Gnome, we believe sovereignty of body and mind cannot be divided.
Your spirit thrives when your body is nourished, your mind is clear, and your soul is honored.
Together they form the living orchard of your being.

Tend all three.
The soil, the branches, the fruit; each is sacred.

Gnome Blessings.

A mirror never lies, but it also never tells the whole story.

It reveals surface, not depth.
It shows form, but not essence.
It catches light, but not the flame that burns within.

This Gnomean Proverb reminds us that truth is layered.
Reflection can be accurate and still incomplete.
To know yourself, you must look beyond the glass into the hidden chambers of the soul.

At the Church of Gnome, we believe self-knowledge is sacred work.
It begins with the mirror, but it cannot end there.
True vision requires both reflection and revelation.

Honor the mirror, but do not mistake it for the whole.
Your depth lies far beyond what it shows.

Gnome Blessings.

You are allowed to end the chapter, even if they won't.

Closure does not wait for someone else's pen.
You can set the book down, turn the page, and begin again.

This Gnomean Proverb reminds us that freedom is not always mutual.
The one who harmed you may cling to the old story, but you are not bound to keep reading it.

At the Church of Gnome, we believe release is a sacred act.
You do not need their permission to walk forward.
You do not need their blessing to find peace.

End the chapter when your spirit is ready.
Let your story continue, whether or not they follow.

Gnome Blessings.

The dawn places a blank page in your hands; what you write today becomes your becoming.

Each sunrise is an unwritten chapter, waiting for the ink of your choices.
Yesterday may linger in memory, but today is the pen that shapes tomorrow.

This Gnomean Proverb reminds us that life is not fixed; it is authored daily.
The smallest words, the quietest decisions, the overlooked gestures all shape who we are becoming.
Every page carries weight, though we rarely see it in the moment.

At the Church of Gnome, we believe the sacred lives in beginnings.
Every dawn is forgiveness.
Every dawn is opportunity.
Every dawn is invitation to write again with greater honesty and deeper love.

Hold the page gently, but do not leave it empty.
Write what matters.
It is becoming you.

Gnome Blessings.

We built ladders to reach the sky, forgetting the stars are also within.

In chasing the heavens, we overlooked the constellations already shining in our own souls.
The cosmos is not only above; it is mirrored in every heart.

This Gnomean Proverb reminds us that seeking outward must be balanced with looking inward.
The external search is noble, but it is incomplete without inner recognition.
The vastness of the universe is echoed in the depth of your being.

At the Church of Gnome, we believe contact with the infinite is not far away.
It is as close as breath, as intimate as silence, as radiant as your own inner spark.

Climb if you must, but do not forget to look inside.
The stars are already there, waiting for you.

Gnome Blessings.

Do not chase joy ahead of you; place it under your feet and let it carry you forward.

We often imagine happiness waiting just beyond reach, tied to what comes next.
But joy is not prize; it is ground.

This Gnomean Proverb reminds us that joy is not something you pursue, but something you stand upon.
It is woven into presence, not pursuit.
When you root yourself in gratitude here, now, the path itself becomes lighter, steadier, sacred.

At the Church of Gnome, we believe joy is not at the end of the road but the road itself.
It is the strength that carries, not the prize that waits.
To walk without it is to stumble.
To walk with it is to already arrive.

Stop chasing.
Step onto joy.
Let it carry you.

Gnome Blessings.

Some throw stones because they can't carry what you hold.

Your light may unsettle those who lost theirs.
Your strength may remind them of what they abandoned.
Your joy may sting in the places they have forgotten to nurture.

This Gnomean Proverb reminds us that cruelty often reveals
more about the one who casts it than the one it strikes.
The stone is their burden, hurled outward because they cannot
bear its weight within.

At the Church of Gnome, we believe the answer to such stones is
not to pick them up and throw them back.
It is to recognize them for what they are; evidence of another's
pain, not proof of your unworthiness.

Stand steady with what you carry.
Do not set it down to ease their envy.
Do not diminish it to soothe their discomfort.

Keep holding the gift that is yours.
Let the stones fall harmless at your feet.

Gnome Blessings.

The mind that bows to another's control forgets its own lantern.

When you hand over your thoughts unexamined, your light dims.
You may carry the lantern still, but it no longer burns with your flame.

This Gnomean Proverb reminds us that sovereignty begins in the mind.
Your lantern was not given to mirror another's path; it was given to guide your own.
To surrender it carelessly is to wander blind, holding light that no longer belongs to you.

At the Church of Gnome, we believe freedom of mind is sacred duty.
Listen, learn, consider; but never surrender the right to question, to discern, to shine your own flame.
The lantern of your thought is your birthright, and no one else may tend it for you.

Guard your mind.
Feed your flame.
Walk with your lantern lit.

Gnome Blessings.

The sharpest wounds are carved not by others, but by thoughts left to wander without watch.

The mind unattended becomes a restless blade, cutting deeper than any enemy could.
Fear, doubt, resentment; these whispers slice from within.

This Gnomean Proverb reminds us that self-harm is not only in body, but in thought.
Neglected, the mind invents injuries that never happened and magnifies the ones that did.
Peace is not taken from us; it is surrendered when we leave our thoughts untended.

At the Church of Gnome, we believe tending the mind is sacred care.
Meditation, reflection, gratitude; these are guards at the gate, keeping the sharp edges from ruling unchecked.
To watch your thoughts is to protect your soul.

Do not leave them unwatched.
They are sharper than you know.

Gnome Blessings.

The veil is thinnest when no one is trying to be important.

Ego builds walls.
Pride makes noise.
But humility opens the quiet space where the unseen can enter.

This Gnomean Proverb reminds us that the sacred often slips in
where striving has ceased.
It reveals itself to the simple, the sincere, the ones willing to
listen instead of perform.

At the Church of Gnome, we believe mystery is not impressed
by status or spectacle.
It meets those who kneel, those who wonder, those who can set
down the need to be significant.

Step gently into the ordinary.
Let your presence be small enough for wonder to notice you.
There, the veil will thin, and you will glimpse what is eternal.

Gnome Blessings.

The meaning of life is not found at the end of the path but in the footprints you leave along the way.

We often imagine purpose waiting like a prize at the finish line, as though meaning were something we will discover only once the journey is over.
But the path does not reveal its secret in endings; it reveals it in each step.

This Gnomean Proverb reminds us that the impressions we leave in the soil of the world are the true measure of our existence.
The kindness we offer, the lessons we share, the small acts of courage and compassion; these are the marks that endure long after the traveler has gone.

At the Church of Gnome, we believe purpose is not a singular revelation but a daily practice.
Meaning grows not in the final destination but in the trail of blessings and burdens you leave behind.

Do not wait for life's end to tell you why you lived.
Look down.
The footprints already hold the answer.

Gnome Blessings.

What was never meant to last still lives in us as if it did.

A fleeting moment can leave roots.
A brief love can linger like eternity.
Even what was temporary can shape us permanently.

This Gnomean Proverb reminds us that impermanence does not mean insignificance.
The short-lived can mark us as deeply as the enduring.
The memory of what passed continues to move within us, shaping who we are.

At the Church of Gnome, we believe time is not the measure of value.
The soul does not count minutes or years; it remembers depth, it remembers meaning, it remembers impact.

Do not dismiss what ended quickly.
It still lives in you, whispering its lesson, carrying its weight, blessing your becoming.

Gnome Blessings.

Every imagined world is a mirror, showing truths our own refuses to speak aloud.

The creatures we invent, the lands we dream, the stories we spin; all carry reflections of ourselves.
Fiction is never only fantasy; it is the soul's way of whispering truths too tender, too daring, or too strange to confess directly.

This Gnomean Proverb reminds us that creation is confession.
The landscapes of imagination reveal what is hidden in the heart: our fears, our hopes, our vision of justice, our longing for connection.
We may call them inventions, but they are revelations.

At the Church of Gnome, we believe storytelling is sacred work.
It allows the soul to speak through masks, to reveal without exposing, to teach without preaching.
Imagined worlds do not hide truth; they frame it so we can finally see.

Pay attention to what you dream.
The mirror is already speaking.

Gnome Blessings.

To stand before beauty is to remember that not all truths can be explained.

A sunrise, a painting, a song that moves you to tears; these moments carry a knowing beyond words.
The heart recognizes what the mind cannot contain.

This Gnomean Proverb reminds us that explanation is not the same as understanding.
Some truths live only in experience.
They cannot be dissected, only received.

At the Church of Gnome, we believe beauty is a form of revelation.
It is the sacred's way of reminding us that not all reality fits in reason's grasp.
To encounter beauty is to bow before mystery, to be humbled by wonder, to be blessed by the ineffable.

Do not demand beauty justify itself.
Let it simply be, and let it teach you.
Some truths are too large for words, but never too small for awe.

Gnome Blessings.

Your weirdness is not a flaw, it's your fingerprint on the sacred.

The parts of you that feel out of step are not mistakes.
They are markers of the holy, proof that the Divine delights in
variety.

This Gnomean Proverb reminds us that difference is not defect;
it is design.
The sacred has no need for copies.
It calls each soul to embody a shape no other could carry.

At the Church of Gnome, we believe uniqueness is a form of
worship.
Your oddness is the color only you can add to creation's canvas.
To hide it is to rob the world of a note in its greater song.

Do not cover your weirdness.
Wear it as a sign that the sacred chose to express itself through
you in a way it never will again.

Gnome Blessings.

The veil is thin in places where hearts are open.

Mystery draws near not because the place is special, but
because the posture is.
Where love softens the walls of the soul, the unseen finds its
doorway.

This Gnomean Proverb reminds us that sacred encounters do
not require temples or rituals alone.
They require openness.
The veil between worlds responds most to hearts that are
willing to welcome.

At the Church of Gnome, we believe reverence is the key that
unlocks contact with the eternal.
The more you open, the more you notice the sacred that was
already surrounding you.
The veil has always been thin; you only needed to soften
enough to see it.

Let your heart open, and the mystery will meet you there.

Gnome Blessings.

Each dilemma is a mirror; what you decide reveals who you are.

We often imagine choices as paths outside ourselves, but in truth they are reflections of what already lives within. When confronted with conflict, the decision exposes the compass of your soul.

This Gnomean Proverb reminds us that moral struggle is less about right and wrong in the abstract, and more about the story you are writing about yourself. Every choice declares what you value, what you fear, and what you are willing to stand for.

At the Church of Gnome, we believe dilemmas are not punishments but invitations. They ask: who are you becoming? They remind us that every action, no matter how small, sculpts the self.

Do not fear the mirror. Look honestly into it. What you choose will reveal the truth of who you are.

Gnome Blessings.

We are not separate stones. We are pieces of the same mountain.

What feels divided is in truth still whole.
Our fractures are the lines where belonging begins.

This Gnomean Proverb reminds us that connection is not a choice, but a reality.
The same forces shaped us, the same ground holds us, the same gravity calls us home.

At the Church of Gnome, we believe unity does not erase individuality.
Each stone keeps its shape, yet all belong to the mountain.
To harm another is to weaken the structure that holds you too.

Remember this when you feel alone.
You are not apart.
You are part of something vast and enduring.

Gnome Blessings.

The gnome does not apologize for dancing.

Joy is not an offense.
Movement is not something to justify.
The sacred delights in bodies moving freely, in spirits
unburdened by shame.

This Gnomean Proverb reminds us that expression is a
birthright.
Celebration needs no permission slip.
Happiness, too, is holy.

At the Church of Gnome, we believe joy is resistance to despair.
It is a testament that life still flows, still sings, still moves
through you despite the world's heaviness.

Dance without apology.
You are not a disruption.
You are proof that the sacred is alive.

Gnome Blessings.

Endurance is sacred, but to worship your wounds is to mistake the bandage for the healing.

Strength is a gift when it carries you through pain.
It becomes a burden when it becomes your identity.

This Gnomean Proverb reminds us that resilience is not meant
to be a throne.
It is meant to be a bridge.
The goal is not to live forever in survival, but to move into
thriving.

At the Church of Gnome, we believe healing means more than
enduring.
It means stepping beyond the wound, letting it close, and living
beyond its narrative.

Honor your endurance.
But when it is time, set it down.
The sacred is not only in the surviving; it is in the becoming
whole again.

Gnome Blessings.

Inquire within, for the garden of your soul cultivates the world around you.

What grows inside spills outward.
Your inner soil becomes the ground others walk on.

This Gnomean Proverb reminds us that the outer world is not
separate from your inner tending.
Bitterness roots outward as thorn.
Peace roots outward as shade.
What you plant inside becomes the harvest others meet.

At the Church of Gnome, we believe self-reflection is not
selfish; it is stewardship.
To tend your inner garden is to bless your community.
To ignore it is to scatter weeds beyond your own walls.

Look inward with care.
The seeds you nurture there will shape the landscape of more
lives than your own.

Gnome Blessings.

Saying no may disappoint others, but it rescues you.

Every yes that betrays your truth is a quiet abandonment of yourself.
Every no spoken with integrity is a rescue mission; your soul reclaiming its ground.

This Gnomean Proverb reminds us that boundaries are not cruelty.
They are lifelines.
They protect your energy, your calling, and your wholeness from being scattered in directions that do not serve your becoming.

At the Church of Gnome, we believe sacred love does not demand self-erasure.
It flows from honesty.
To give without truth is to give poisoned water.
To say no with sincerity is to leave space for your yes to matter again.

Disappointment will pass.
But the soul you rescue will remain with you forever.

Gnome Blessings.

To meet anxiety with resistance is to wrestle smoke; to meet it with breath is to open a window.

Fear tightens when fought.
Panic swells when named enemy.
But the breath loosens the knot, reminding the body that there is space, that there is air, that there is life beyond the moment.

This Gnomean Proverb reminds us that anxiety is not conquered through force.
It is softened through presence.
Breath becomes the doorway where tension finds its release.

At the Church of Gnome, we believe the spirit is braided into the body.
When the body calms, the soul remembers its center.
When breath is chosen, fear loses its grip.

Do not wrestle the smoke.
Open the window.
Let the breath carry you back into peace.

Gnome Blessings.

Your rhythm is not wrong, it's just not theirs.

You are not broken for moving slower, nor flawed for running faster.
Your pace belongs to your path, shaped by your story, your body, your soul.

This Gnomean Proverb reminds us that comparison distorts truth.
The drumbeat of your life was never meant to match the march of another.
Your timing is sacred, even when misunderstood.

At the Church of Gnome, we believe harmony is not sameness.
The world's song requires many rhythms, many tempos, many movements woven together.
Your cadence belongs in the music, just as it is.

Trust the beat that lives within you.
It may be the rhythm another soul has been waiting to hear.

Gnome Blessings.

Your difference is not a burden, it is your beacon.

The parts of you that do not blend in were never meant to.
They were meant to shine, to signal, to call others out of their hiding.

This Gnomean Proverb reminds us that what isolates you in one place may illuminate you in another.
Your difference is the lighthouse guiding those searching for kinship.

At the Church of Gnome, we believe every soul carries a flame of uniqueness.
When hidden, the world grows dim.
When revealed, the world grows brighter.
To live fully is to let your beacon shine unapologetically.

Do not shrink to ease the comfort of others.
Stand tall.
Your light is not weight; it is invitation.

Gnome Blessings.

The soul, like the soil, changes in cycles.

Seasons of fertility give way to seasons of rest.
Times of abundance are followed by fallow ground.
Nothing in nature is constant, and neither are you.

This Gnomean Proverb reminds us that change is not failure,
but rhythm.
Your soul is not meant to be in endless bloom.
It is meant to rest, to renew, to prepare for its next becoming.

At the Church of Gnome, we believe patience with yourself is
sacred.
To honor your cycles is to live in harmony with the earth.
The soil knows when to pause.
The soul knows too, if you allow it.

Trust your seasons.
They are not setbacks.
They are sacred spirals of becoming.

Gnome Blessings.

What we chase often circles back behind us, laughing at the pursuit.

Desire convinces us that fulfillment lies just ahead, always a little farther, always a little out of reach.
Yet when we grasp for it, we find it was never in the distance; it was waiting quietly within.

This Gnomean Proverb reminds us that irony is the teacher of humility.
We spend lifetimes in pursuit of things that arrive only once we stop running.
Happiness, peace, meaning; these do not live in the horizon but in the soil beneath our own feet.

At the Church of Gnome, we believe the trickster is sacred, for it teaches us to laugh at our seriousness.
Life is not mocked in cruelty, but in kindness; reminding us that what we sought was never missing, only misplaced.

Pause in your chasing.
Turn around.
The thing you long for may already be standing there, smiling at your pursuit.

Gnome Blessings.

The gnome learns most from what he cannot name.

Mystery is the greatest teacher.
The ungraspable, the unspoken, the undefined; these carry
truths too vast for language.

This Gnomean Proverb reminds us that wisdom does not
always come through clarity.
Sometimes it comes through awe.
Sometimes it comes through reverence for what cannot be held.

At the Church of Gnome, we believe the unknown is not a
threat, but a gift.
The mind longs to label, but the soul longs to bow.
It is in the space of not-knowing that we grow most deeply.

Do not fear what you cannot name.
Let it teach you.
Let it humble you.
Let it make you whole.

Gnome Blessings.

You are not less sacred for being mistaken.

Error does not cancel essence.
Wrong turns do not erase the map within you.
Even the missteps are part of the sacred choreography of your
becoming.

This Gnomean Proverb reminds us that perfection is not a
prerequisite for holiness.
Mistakes are not stains; they are teachers, shaping humility,
empathy, and depth of character.
What you regret today may become the soil of your wisdom
tomorrow.

At the Church of Gnome, we believe the sacred does not
withdraw from you when you falter.
It walks with you through the misstep, guiding you back to
yourself.
To be human is to err.
To be sacred is to grow.

Do not shrink when you fall short.
You are still a vessel of light, still worthy of reverence.

Gnome Blessings.

When your animal looks at you, the universe does too.

In that gaze lives the whole of creation: trust, dependence,
wildness, and quiet knowing.
It is not just eyes meeting eyes.
It is existence recognizing itself across different forms.

This Gnomean Proverb reminds us that animals are not beneath
us but beside us.
They carry the same breath, the same stardust, the same
mysterious spark.
Their presence reflects back the parts of us we forget:
innocence, loyalty, presence, and unspoken truth.

At the Church of Gnome, we believe our companions are sacred
mirrors.
Their devotion is not simple instinct; it is a living hymn.
When they look at you, the universe witnesses the bond.

Meet their gaze with reverence.
There is more looking through their eyes than you can imagine.

Gnome Blessings.

Trying to control the wind just makes you look dramatic.

The currents move where they will.
Your grasping does not stop them.
It only exhausts you, making a spectacle of your resistance.

This Gnomean Proverb reminds us that some forces are not meant to be managed.
Life has its own weather, its own seasons, its own gusts and calms.
You cannot command them.
You can only adjust your sails and let them teach you.

At the Church of Gnome, we believe wisdom lies not in controlling, but in responding.
When you release the illusion of control, you find the freedom of movement.
You discover that surrender is not weakness; it is alignment.

Stop wrestling the wind.
Let it guide you instead.

Gnome Blessings.

The weight of existence presses hardest just before awe breaks through.

Dread may feel like a crushing silence, an emptiness that
stretches too far to bear.
But often that heaviness is the threshold, the soul bracing itself
before mystery is revealed.

This Gnomean Proverb reminds us that the questions that
terrify us are often the very questions that prepare us for
wonder.
The shiver of meaninglessness is not the end; it is the clearing
away of illusions that no longer serve.
Awe enters through the cracks dread leaves behind.

At the Church of Gnome, we believe despair is not always
destruction; it can be preparation.
The night feels longest just before dawn.
The burden of existence presses hardest just before the heart
learns to expand and receive the immensity of being alive.

When dread arrives, do not turn away.
Stay long enough to see what follows.
Awe is already waiting at the edges of your fear.

Gnome Blessings.

You are not who you were. That is proof the ritual worked.

The old self has been shed, like a snake leaving its skin on the forest floor.
You carry its memory, but not its weight.
What once defined you now lies behind you, a relic of the journey already passed.

This Gnomean Proverb reminds us that transformation is not always loud.
Sometimes it is as subtle as noticing you no longer respond with the same fear, no longer cling to the same wound, no longer kneel before the same false altar.
The ritual; whether through fire, through silence, through grief, through joy; does not leave you as it found you.

At the Church of Gnome, we believe rituals are not empty motions but catalysts.
They mark the threshold where the old dissolves and the new is born.
You may not feel the change in the moment, but the proof is in the becoming.
The person you are now is the testimony that the sacred work was real.

Do not long for the one you used to be.
That self did its part and released you into this one.
The ritual has done its work.
The transformation is already alive in you.

Gnome Blessings.

One lantern in the dark is enough to reveal the cowardice of the crowd.

The faintest flame shatters the illusion that nothing can be seen.
It proves that the night was never as absolute as fear claimed.

This Gnomean Proverb reminds us that courage is contagious, and that often it takes only one act of light to expose the excuses of many.
The crowd may hide in shadows, claiming safety, but the lantern-bearer reveals that fear was their choice, not their fate.

At the Church of Gnome, we believe one voice, one act, one light is enough to transform a space of silence.
The lantern-bearer is not greater than the crowd, but truer.
They refuse to surrender to darkness simply because others did.

Do not underestimate the power of your flame.
It may shame those who hid.
It may inspire those who doubted.
It may guide those who were waiting for a single spark to remind them of their own fire.

In every age, the night grows thick, and in every age, one lantern proves it cannot last.
Carry the light.
It is always enough.

Gnome Blessings.

Every decision is a thread.

It ties not only to your own life, but to the lives around you.
It weaves into a fabric larger than you will ever see.

This Gnomean Proverb reminds us that our choices ripple
outward.
What you do in secret still touches others.
What you do in the open still returns to you.
No act is isolated.

At the Church of Gnome, we believe that life is an interwoven
tapestry.
Your joy creates space for another's joy.
Your harm creates wounds that may bleed beyond your
knowing.
You do not walk alone, even when you feel solitary.

Every choice is both personal and communal.
To choose well is to honor the whole, not just the self.
To live awake is to remember that you are part of something
greater.

The story is not yours alone.
It belongs to the web you are helping to create.

Gnome Blessings.

Let joy feel normal again.

Do not treat it as rare, fragile, or undeserved.
Joy is not a visitor that comes only once in a while.
It is woven into the fabric of life, waiting for permission to stay.

This Gnomean Proverb reminds us that suffering often feels
familiar, while joy feels foreign.
We brace for its departure instead of settling into its presence.
But joy was never meant to be rationed; it was meant to flow.

At the Church of Gnome, we believe joy is sacred inheritance.
It belongs not only to moments of triumph but to the ordinary
rhythms of breath, meal, laughter, and touch.
To normalize joy is to honor its holiness, to let it be part of the
everyday ground of being.

Let yourself trust it.
Let yourself rest in it.
Joy is not a trick of the moment; it is the truth that has been
here all along.

Gnome Blessings.

Step forward even if the ground hasn't appeared yet.

Faith often arrives in motion.
The path builds itself under the weight of your courage.

This Gnomean Proverb reminds us that waiting for certainty often means waiting forever.
The unknown does not reveal itself until you risk the step.
Your trust creates the ground where fear insisted there was only emptiness.

At the Church of Gnome, we believe courage is the architect of new worlds.
Each step forward is a prayer, a declaration that life is trustworthy even when it feels hidden.
What looks like a void may already be waiting to become your path.

Do not demand to see the entire road.
Take the step.
The earth will rise to meet you.

Gnome Blessings.

We remember in symbols, not facts. That's how the soul speaks.

A scent pulls back a lifetime.
A melody brings a forgotten season to the surface.
The soul arranges memory not as ledger, but as altar, built from signs and echoes.

This Gnomean Proverb reminds us that truth is carried more by meaning than by detail.
Facts fade and shift, but the symbols remain; doors, rivers, lanterns, faces; each one holding more weight than any list of dates or numbers.

At the Church of Gnome, we believe symbols are sacred language.
They bypass the mind and speak directly to the spirit.
To remember through symbols is to remember through poetry, through essence, through what the heart has always known.

Pay attention to what returns to you in symbol.
It is the soul reminding you of what still matters.

Gnome Blessings.

What we refuse to see in ourselves, others are forced to carry.

Denial never dissolves a burden; it simply shifts the weight to those near us.
Our shadows do not disappear. They spill outward.

This Gnomean Proverb reminds us that avoidance creates collateral damage.
The pain you hide in silence leaks into your words, your choices, your relationships.
Others end up holding what you refuse to name.

At the Church of Gnome, we believe responsibility is sacred.
To face yourself is to free others from carrying what was always yours.
Healing is never only for you; it is mercy for those around you.

See yourself honestly.
What you acknowledge can be healed.
What you deny will become someone else's burden.

Gnome Blessings.

Freedom is not the absence of path, but the courage to walk it awake.

We imagine freedom as limitless choice, a blank field with no boundaries.
But even in endless fields, you must choose a direction, and every choice carries consequence.

This Gnomean Proverb reminds us that true freedom is not about escape; it is about awareness.
It is the ability to see the path you are on, to own it, to walk it without sleepwalking through borrowed decisions or inherited fears.

At the Church of Gnome, we believe freedom is both gift and responsibility.
The path may be shaped by forces beyond us: history, chance, mystery, but our freedom lies in how we walk it: with intention, with courage, with awake eyes.

Do not seek a life without path.
Seek instead to walk your path awake, step by step, with sovereignty of body and mind.

Gnome Blessings.

You cannot carry the forest with you. But you can carry its song.

The trees will not fit into your arms.
The moss will not stay on your shoes.
Yet the memory of its silence and its song lives within you
wherever you go.

This Gnomean Proverb reminds us that belonging to the earth
does not mean possession.
It means remembering, echoing, honoring what you
experienced when you were among it.

At the Church of Gnome, we believe the forest does not ask to be
owned.
It asks to be carried in the way you live, the way you speak, the
way you breathe.
Its song in your heart is enough to keep you connected.

Leave the forest as it is.
Carry its music instead.
That is how reverence travels.

Gnome Blessings.

Your worth is not what they see, but what you carry unseen.

The world may judge by surface, by polish, by noise.
But the unseen; your endurance, your kindness, your inner fire;
holds the greater weight.

This Gnomean Proverb reminds us that the sacred often hides
within.
True worth is not display, but essence.
It is the quiet choices, the private integrity, the unseen courage
that no crowd applauds.

At the Church of Gnome, we believe dignity is rooted in what
cannot be measured by sight.
Your hidden light does not depend on recognition to be real.
It burns steadily whether or not anyone notices.

Carry your unseen worth proudly.
It is your truest treasure.

Gnome Blessings.

To move as one is to glimpse the larger spirit we already belong to.

When voices rise together, when hands join, when hearts align, something greater than the sum of us emerges.
It is not created in that moment; it is revealed.

This Gnomean Proverb reminds us that community is not an invention, but a remembering.
We already belong to something vast and interconnected; collective joy and unity simply awaken us to what has always been true.

At the Church of Gnome, we believe sacredness often appears in circles; dances, songs, rituals, shared meals.
In these moments, individuality is not erased, but woven into harmony.
Each person remains themselves, yet contributes to a spirit larger than themselves.

When you move as one, do not dismiss it as fleeting emotion.
It is a glimpse of reality itself: you are part of something infinite.
The larger spirit was always there; you only had to join the circle to feel it.

Gnome Blessings.

The question is the altar. The asking is the offering.

Every time you step into uncertainty with humility, you kneel at something sacred.
You admit that you are small before mystery, that your mind cannot hold all of it, and yet your heart still reaches.

This Gnomean Proverb reminds us that prayer does not always wear the shape of answers.
It often takes the form of open hands, of wondering aloud, of surrendering certainty in exchange for connection.
The altar is not built from marble or stone; it is built every time a question is carried with reverence instead of scorn.

At the Church of Gnome, we believe the sacred listens more closely to curiosity than to pride.
The act of asking, when done honestly, is itself devotion.
The question itself becomes a bridge, carrying you from what you know into what you long to know.
The silence that follows the asking is not absence; it is invitation, a space where wonder lingers.

Do not be ashamed of your questions.
They are not proof of ignorance, but proof of reverence.
To ask sincerely is to offer the truest gift you can give: your vulnerability, your openness, your readiness to be changed.

Kneel at the altar of your questions.
Let the offering be your wonder.
That alone is holy.

Gnome Blessings.

To delight in cruelty is to dim your own lantern.

The moment you savor another's pain, the flame within you
falters.
What seems like power is only shadow; what feels like victory is
only smoke.

This Gnomean Proverb reminds us that cruelty corrodes the soul of
the one who wields it.
The lantern is built for light, for guidance, for warmth.
When cruelty is entertained, soot gathers on the glass, and soon
the light cannot shine clearly.

At the Church of Gnome, we believe joy at another's suffering is
not strength, but decay.
The sacred spark within every being is dimmed when we celebrate
harm.
The soul shrinks when laughter feeds on pain, when satisfaction
comes from another's fall.
That is not justice. That is hunger disguised as triumph.

Guard your lantern.
Do not let cruelty touch its flame.
Choose compassion even when anger tempts you toward hardness.
Choose mercy even when bitterness insists you strike.
In protecting your light, you preserve the truth of who you are.

The world needs your lantern bright, not clouded by malice.
Shine in a way that heals.
Shine in a way that warms.
Let cruelty find no home in you.

Gnome Blessings.

You will outgrow even the pain that taught you to grow.

The wound may have shaped you, but it was never meant to hold you forever.
Its lessons are real, but they are not your final name.

This Gnomean Proverb reminds us that healing is not only about enduring suffering; it is about moving beyond its claim on your identity.
Pain is a teacher, but teachers are not meant to keep students captive.
Growth continues long after the wound has closed.

At the Church of Gnome, we believe gratitude for what pain revealed can coexist with release from its grip.
You can honor what it showed you without binding yourself to its memory.
You can carry the wisdom forward while laying the ache to rest.

Do not mistake the teacher for the destination.
You are more than what hurt you.
You are the growth that sprang from it, and the freedom that follows.

Gnome Blessings.

The garden grows without your grip.

You may plant, you may water, you may tend, but growth is not yours to force.
Life unfolds in its own time, regardless of how tightly you try to control it.

This Gnomean Proverb reminds us that obsession with outcomes robs us of reverence for process.
To grip too tightly is to strangle what was meant to breathe.
The garden does not need clenched fists; it needs open hands, patient eyes, and trust in the unseen work beneath the soil.

At the Church of Gnome, we believe creation responds to partnership, not domination.
We are co-tenders, not commanders.
The mystery of growth has always belonged to forces larger than us; sun, rain, soil, time.
Our task is not to control, but to align.

Release your grip.
Do the work, then step back.
Let the garden grow as it was always meant to; freely, abundantly, in its own rhythm.

Gnome Blessings.

You cannot outrun what waits patiently within.

The faster you flee, the closer it follows.
Shadows do not vanish with speed; they walk quietly until you
are too tired to resist.

This Gnomean Proverb reminds us that avoidance never brings
freedom.
The self you deny does not disappear.
The grief, the fear, the truth you bury simply settles deeper,
waiting with patience to be met.

At the Church of Gnome, we believe healing is not found in
escape but in embrace.
To stop running is to discover that what chased you was never a
predator, but a part of you longing to be seen.
When you finally turn to face it, it loses its threat and becomes
your companion, your teacher, your hidden strength.

Do not wear yourself out on endless paths of denial.
Sit down.
Let what waits within catch up.
Its presence may be the very thing that makes you whole.

Gnome Blessings.

There are truths the sun is too loud to tell.

Some revelations require shadows, silence, and the softened
light of dusk.
The bright glare hides as much as it reveals, washing over the
subtler shapes.

This Gnomean Proverb reminds us that wisdom has its seasons.
The loudness of the day illuminates action, but the quiet of
night uncovers secrets.
Not every truth announces itself with brilliance; some whisper
only in stillness.

At the Church of Gnome, we believe listening requires patience
for the conditions that truth demands.
The sun tells its truths of clarity and exposure, but the moon
tells the truths of intimacy, reflection, and the mysteries that
cannot survive harsh light.
To honor truth is to wait for it in its chosen hour.

Sit in the twilight.
Let the quiet truths emerge.
They will reveal what the sun could not say.

Gnome Blessings.

You can't sage away what still controls your choices.

Rituals may cleanse the air, but they cannot erase what is rooted deep in the soul.
The smoke may carry prayers upward, but healing requires your willingness to look inward.

This Gnomean Proverb reminds us that sacred practice is not substitution for transformation.
Tools can aid you, but they cannot replace the work of honesty.
Until you name what binds you, no flame or fragrance will set you free.

At the Church of Gnome, we believe ritual is powerful when it is paired with intention.
To burn sage or lift incense is meaningful only when you are ready to confront the truth that lingers behind the smoke.
The work is both outer and inner; sacred action joined to sacred courage.

Do not mistake ceremony for completion.
Face what controls you.
Only then will the ritual become real.

Gnome Blessings.

Your weirdness is your holiness peeking through.

The crooked laugh, the odd delight, the way you see the world at an angle no one else notices; these are not flaws to conceal. They are the fingerprints of the sacred, reminding you that you were never meant to blend into sameness.

This Gnomean Proverb reminds us that holiness is not sterile, polished, or uniform.
It is vibrant, strange, and alive.
It wears disguises of eccentricity, quirks, and unconventional vision.
What others call weird is often the precise place where the sacred has broken through the ordinary veil and left its mark on you.

At the Church of Gnome, we believe the sacred delights in difference.
The Divine has no need for duplicates.
Each life is crafted as a singular expression of wonder, carrying a light no other can hold.
To hide that light is not humility; it is theft, robbing the world of the blessing that only you can offer.

Do not apologize for the shape of your soul.
Do not cover your oddness as though it were shameful.
It is your holiness slipping into view, reminding you and the world that the sacred prefers diversity over uniformity, play over perfection.

Your weirdness is your gift.
Let it shine without disguise.

Gnome Blessings.

Final Benediction

This book is not an end,
but an opening.
The words you have received are not finished.
They are alive.
They wait now in you,
ready to be carried into the world.

The Church of Gnome proclaims:
that wisdom is sown in every corner of existence;
that no soil is too poor to bear truth,
no heart too broken to cradle light.
We proclaim that the sacred is not distant,
but near;
hidden in gardens and kitchens,
in song and silence,
in laughter that startles the night,
in tears that water the ground,
in creatures small and great,
in mysteries too wide for our grasp.

The proverbs given here are lanterns.
They are not lit for one alone.
They are lit for the path we share,
for companions known and unknown,
for the weary and the seeking,
for the generations who will walk after us.
They are entrusted now to you.

Therefore, carry them:
not as commandments carved in stone,
but as living sparks.
Let them kindle gratitude when you wake.
Let them steady you when shadows lengthen.
Let them soften your heart when anger hardens.
Let them call you back when you forget who you are.

The Church of Gnome is not a fortress,
but a circle.
It is not a demand,
but an invitation.
Its gates stand open to all who desire peace,
all who seek meaning without chains,
all who wish to walk with reverence and with joy.
It is a fellowship that honors difference,
that defends the sovereignty of body and mind,
that blesses the companionship of animals,
that holds both absurdity and awe as sacred teachers.

If your spirit has stirred in these pages,
know that the circle is waiting.
Come to **www.ChurchOfGnome.org**.
Step into a community of seekers across the earth.
Join in membership if you desire belonging.
Or simply walk with us as a friend of the garden.
The lanterns multiply when shared.
The circle grows with every heart that enters.

And now receive this blessing:

May your roots be deep,
drawing strength from the hidden places.
May your branches be wide,
giving shelter to those who rest in your shade.
May your mind be clear as running water,
and your spirit vast as the open sky.
May your labor bear fruit,
and your rest restore you.
May your companions; human and creature;
walk with you in trust and joy.
May your laughter keep you light,
and your tears keep you tender.
May wonder never leave your eyes,
and courage never leave your steps.

And may you always remember:
The light entrusted to you is not yours alone.
The light of one lantern does not diminish another.
It only makes the path brighter.

Go now as bearer of that light.
Go as guardian of gardens,
as seeker of mystery,
as companion to all who walk beside you.
For the story is not finished.
It begins again in you.

Gnome Blessings